Joseph George Rosengarten

The German Soldier in the Wars of the United States

Vol. 1

Joseph George Rosengarten

The German Soldier in the Wars of the United States
Vol. 1

ISBN/EAN: 9783337308100

Printed in Europe, USA, Canada, Australia, Japan

Cover: Foto ©ninafisch / pixelio.de

More available books at **www.hansebooks.com**

THE GERMAN SOLDIER

IN THE

WARS OF THE UNITED STATES.

BY

J. G. ROSENGARTEN.

PHILADELPHIA:
J. B. LIPPINCOTT COMPANY.
1886.

In Memory

OF

ADOLPH G. ROSENGARTEN,

Major 15th Pennsylvania (Anderson) Cavalry,

Born in Philadelphia, December 29, 1838; Killed in Battle at Stone River, Tennessee, December 29, 1862.

PREFATORY NOTE.

THE substance of the following pages was read before the Pionier Verein at the hall of the German Society, in Philadelphia, April 21, 1885. It was printed with some changes in the *United Service* Magazine of New York, in the numbers for June, July, and August, 1885, and it was translated and printed in German in full in the *Nebraska Tribune*, in successive issues, between June 20th and October 27, 1885,—the last number being a supplementary article by the translator, Fr. Schnake, on the German Soldiers of the Border States. It was subsequently published in a pamphlet of forty-nine pages by J. B. Lippincott Company, Philadelphia, for the Pionier Verein. That edition is exhausted, and in reply to numerous applications, showing interest in the subject, it is now reprinted with many corrections and considerable additions. For these the author is indebted most of all to the *Deutsche Pionier* of Cincinnati and to the editor, H. A. Ratterman, the best authority on all subjects concerning the Germans of the United States,—and among others to Mr. F. Melchers, of the *Deutsche Zeitung*, Charleston, South Carolina; Mr. Herman Dieck, of the *German Demokrat*, Philadelphia; General Lewis Merrill, U.S.A.; Colonel John P. Nicholson, Dr. J. de B. W. Gardiner, U.S.A.; Prof. O. Seidensticker, of the University of Pennsylvania, and Mr. George M. Abbot, of the Philadelphia Library,—his " Bibliography of the Civil War in the United States" is indispensable for a student of our military history. Whatever there is of merit or interest in these pages is largely due to the assistance thus liberally given. With further aid in the way either of corrections or additions, which will be gladly received and gratefully acknowledged, the author of this sketch hopes that he may hereafter be enabled to make it better worth the interest of the reader and the importance of the subject.

J. G. R.

PHILADELPHIA, April 21, 1886,
532 WALNUT STREET.

THE GERMAN SOLDIER

IN THE

WARS OF THE UNITED STATES.

THE share of the Germans in the wars of the United States is by no means limited to that of the Rebellion. From the very outset of their settlement in the country they always stood ready to take their place in its defence. On the borders of what was then the West, the early German immigrants were steady in their support of the British flag against their hereditary enemies, the French. This was natural enough, for many of the Germans who first came to this country did so in order to seek refuge from the French invaders, who rode rough-shod over their humble homes in the districts of Germany devastated by French soldiers. Even among those who came here to find a new home in which they could worship God in their own way, while they sympathized with the Quakers in their doctrine of not bearing arms voluntarily, the German blood did not easily accommodate itself to the doctrine of non-resistance, and when they could not make friends of the Indians by peaceful means, the German settlers did not hesitate to take up arms in defence of their homes. The Germans of Pennsylvania and New York responded freely to the summons to defend their new country against the French and their allies, the Indians. They gave freely of their men and their means to the cause of liberty in the war of the Revolution. They took a full share in the war of 1812, and in the Mexican war. Finally, wherever the Germans were strongest in number, they were represented in even more than proportionate strength in the forces raised for the defence of the Union. From New York and Pennsylvania they went forth in great strength in regiments and individually. They saved Missouri to the Union, and Ohio and Illinois and Indiana and Wisconsin and Kansas may well point with pride to their German citizens as foremost in doing their duty in war and in peace. The story of their achievements in war is a subject on which little has hitherto been said.

The Germans from the Palatinate had been scattered on the frontier, facing the Indians and the French in New York and Pennsylvania. The early settlers in South and North Carolina and Georgia were also largely recruited from the Germans, and they, too, had still another hostile force to meet, that of the Spanish troops and Indians, whose masters were unwilling to see their territory threatened and diminished. The good Moravians gave up their settlements in Georgia rather than fight, and thus lost the fruits of some years of labor in their schools and churches. The sturdy Protestants from the Palatinate were not afraid to take up arms in defence of their own homes, and in a very short time the British government, which had brought them here as an act of benevolence, found a good return in the services rendered by the German settlers as peacemakers with the Indians, and when necessary, as soldiers against the French and the Spanish and their native allies. There was, indeed, quite a characteristic jealousy of them on the part of their unwarlike neighbors in Pennsylvania, and not a little of the hostility which marked the treatment of the early German settlers in New York was due to their sturdy indifference to those, both Dutch and English, the great land-owners, who would have controlled them and used them as feudal serfs. They acknowledged their allegiance to the crown, and gladly served it. They refused to submit to the tyranny of great landlords, and on that account soon left New York to find permanent homes under the kindlier sway of the Penns. Pennsylvania made Conrad Weiser colonel of a regiment of volunteers from the county of Berks, and Governor Morris, in 1755, gave him command over the second battalion of the Pennsylvania regiment, consisting of nine companies. In the defence of the borders against the Indians and the French, forts were built by the German settlers above Harrisburg, at the forks of the Schuylkill, on the Lehigh, and on the Upper Delaware. The Hon. Daniel Ermentrout, in his address at the German Centennial Jubilee in Reading in June, 1876, describes the Tulpehocken massacre in 1755, just after Braddock's defeat, the barbarities perpetrated in Northampton County in 1756, and the attack on the settlements near Reading in 1763. Against these forays the Germans under Schneider and

Hiester made a stout resistance. As early as 1711 a German battalion, mainly natives of the Palatinate, was part of the force, a thousand strong, which was to take part in the expedition to Quebec. While the Quakers of Pennsylvania kept the government from exerting its full strength, the Germans, in spite of their peace principles, stood up stoutly for their own homesteads. Berks, Bucks, Lancaster, York, and Northampton were then the frontier counties, and from them came the men who filled the German regiments and battalions of the Revolutionary war. The sufferings inflicted on the German settlers were not without their influence in inspiring their descendants with the patriotism which made them good soldiers both in the Revolution and in the war of the Rebellion.

At the outbreak of the old French war, the British government, under an act of Parliament passed for the purpose, organized the Royal American Regiment for service in the colonies. This force was to consist of four battalions, of one thousand men each. Fifty of the officers were to be foreign Protestants, while the enlisted men were to be raised principally from among the German settlers in America. The immediate commander,

General Bouquet, was a Swiss by birth, an English officer by adoption, and a Pennsylvanian by naturalization. This last distinction was conferred on him in compliment, and as a reward for his services in his campaigns in the western part of Pennsylvania, where he and his Germans atoned for the injuries that resulted from Braddock's defeat in the same border region.*

The first colonel of the regiment was Lord Loudoun, and the four battalions were commanded by Stanwix, Duffeaux, Jeffereys, and Provost. Lord Howe was commissioned colonel in 1757, when he was first ordered to America. The regiment itself still exists as the Sixtieth of the line of the British army. Bouquet himself died in 1765, at Pensacola, just after he had received the thanks of the Assembly of Pennsylvania for his victory at Bushy Run in 1763. It was to the Germans of his force that is due much of the credit of this action, making amends for the disaster of Braddock's defeat. A chaplain of this regiment, who shared in its

---

* One of the best evidences of the interest taken in this organization is the sermon preached in Christ Church, Philadelphia, by the Rev. Dr. William Smith, which was printed at the request of the colonel and officers.

operations at Louisburg and on the frontiers, the Rev. Michael Schlattler, died at Chestnut Hill, Philadelphia, in 1790, in the enjoyment of a pension from the British government, although he had proved himself a good patriot in the Revolutionary war. His descendants were well known as successful merchants in Philadelphia, while his own memory is honored by a biography giving an account of his varied services to the Church.

But from the Germans of Pennsylvania there went forth an influence among the Indians more potential in saving the country from desolating border warfare than soldiers or fortifications. While the French were striving to make the Indians their allies in war, the Germans, and especially the Moravians, were working successfully to convert the savages into peaceful Christians, and make them good neighbors, useful and obedient to the authorities, and a strong defence against the inroads of their more savage brethren influenced by the French. The Moravians sent their members out to preserve peace; their knowledge of the Indians and their languages, their intercourse and intermarriages, had secured the confidence of the untutored savages. Parkman, in his last work, "Montcalm and Wolfe in the French War of 1759," describes at length the mission undertaken by Christian Frederick Post as envoy to the hostile tribes on the distant Ohio.* The Moravians were apostles of peace, and they succeeded to a surprising degree in weaning their Indian converts from their ferocious instincts and warlike habits. Post boldly presented himself among those who were still savage, and his first reception was by a crowd of warriors, their faces distorted with rage, threatening to kill him. Soon after the French offered a great reward for his scalp, but Post, undaunted, declared to the Indians the coming of an army to drive off the French, and in return received the promise of the warlike savages to keep the peace. After a conference at Easton, Post again went on a mission of peace to the tribes of the Ohio. The small escort of soldiers that attended him as far as the Allegheny, was cut to pieces on its return

---

* Frederick Post was a German Moravian, who, as early as 1761, settled in what is now Bethlehem Township, Stark County, Ohio, where he built a block-house and cleared a few acres of forest, and established a mission settlement. The family of Heckewelder joined him there, but later settled at Gnadenhütten in Tuscarawas County. The site of the former is marked by a few remains of the old block-house.

by a band of the very warriors to whom he was carrying his offers of friendship. His overtures were accepted, and the Delawares, Shawnees, and Mingoes ceased to be enemies. The English soldiers failed by force of arms to accomplish what the German missionary had successfully attained. Thus the work of the Moravians in their quiet home at Bethlehem had enabled their representative to gain the friendship and alliance of the Indians, and to weaken the force of the French and proportionately strengthen that of the English, and this was in no small degree an important factor in the final overthrow of the French in America.

In Kapp's "History of the Early German Settlers of New York," we find the names of the first German soldiers, those who bore arms in defence of their hardly-won homesteads against the French and their allies, the Indians. Among them were the Weisers, father and son. The elder, John Conrad, born in Würtemberg, came to this country a few years after his native village was burned by the French in their invasion in 1693, and died in Pennsylvania in 1746, where he and other German settlers found refuge from the unfair treatment of the wealthy New York land-owners. Conrad Weiser, his son, born in 1696 in Germany, came, with his father, as a boy to New York, and after a brief experience of border-life with the German settlers west of the Hudson, lived with the Indians long enough to be their fast friend, and to serve as their intermediary with the whites, helping thus to preserve the peace in the midst of hostile influences. He died near Reading, in 1760. As lieutenant-colonel of a Pennsylvania regiment he shared in the hardships of the "old French war," and secured from the allied Indians an affection and respect which stood his fellow-Germans in good stead in later years. His daughter was the wife of the elder Muhlenberg, the first of that name to come to this country, and the mother of General Muhlenberg of Revolutionary fame.

As early as 1711 the elder Weiser had led his German countrymen in an expedition to Canada, in defence of the English against the French; and the younger Weiser, in 1737, boldly went out among the wild tribes of native Indians and successfully brought them to make peace with the new settlers. In 1748 he penetrated the unknown country west as far as the Ohio, and in 1754 he united the friendly Indians in a strong alliance, which served very greatly to resist the French intrigues and invasions.

During the Revolutionary war, while many of the Germans of New York were serving in the army, their homes and those of their neighbors were exposed to the attacks of savage enemies, French and Indians rivalling one another in cruelties. The German settlers and their families defended themselves with real courage, and the story of their heroic deeds well deserves the lasting record that Kapp has secured it in his interesting volume. The border warfare, of what was then Western New York, showed that among the Germans there were many stout hearts and strong hands ready to defend their lives and to protect their families. Each home was a block-house and every fort a gathering-point, yet the English were as bitter in repressing the liberty-loving Germans as ever the French had been in attacking them for their loyalty to England. Even when the war ended it was with a sacrifice of lives and property that fell heavily on the German settlers. All this, however, was a training and experience that helped to make them devoted patriots, and earnest in their readiness to sacrifice everything in defence of their newly-acquired liberty and independence. From the same counties came many regiments into the army that helped to defend and preserve the

Union, and although the distinctive German characteristics were less marked in New York than in Pennsylvania, still a military history of New York in the Rebellion, whenever it is written, will show that the Germans, descendants of the early Pfaslzers and Rhinelanders, who had settled in New York in the early part of the eighteenth century, were fully alive to the patriotic demand made upon them in the middle of the nineteenth century.

In 1728, the first conflict in Pennsylvania took place between Germans and Indians at Manatawny. In 1755, after Braddock's defeat, the Indians attacked the Moravian settlements, and all the frontier counties were ravaged by them. Franklin himself headed a regiment in defence of Pennsylvania, in which many Germans served, and he gave them hearty praise for their bravery. When another outbreak occurred in 1763, Bouquet with his regiment of Royal Americans, officered as well as manned by Germans, put it down. The Germans of Charleston, South Carolina, organized in 1775 a Fusilier Company, which served through the Revolution and is still in existence. In Georgia many of the early German settlers enlisted under General Wayne in the Revolutionary army.

The German soldier has gone through all the phases of history in our brief experience of war. In the Revolution the Hessians became a by-word, and yet they were rather the victims of political evils than willing partisans. Not the least of Friederich Kapp's great services to both the country of his adoption and that of his nativity, is his series of admirable works on the German soldiers of the Revolution, on the one side, his account of the dealings in them as mercenaries, and on the other, his lives of Steuben and De Kalb. Much of his material has supplied that for later authors, notably Green and Lowell. Von Elking has furnished the story of Riedesel's life, the commander of the German forces in the British army. The "Memoirs of Mme. von Riedesel" will always be read with interest as a picture of the times of the Revolution, both in Germany and in America.

The material for a statistical account of the German forces engaged in America has been found in the well-ordered and well-preserved archives of the various German states from which they came. For our "War of the Rebellion" such data are not easily attainable. The story covers too vast a field to be briefly told. The method of raising troops in the separate States obliges an inquirer to make an examination of the printed records of each State, and these are so voluminous and so unsystematic, that it is almost impossible to get at the facts of the nativity of the soldiers serving in their organizations. Indeed, there still remains to be written a history of the part of New York in the war, and in those bulky volumes of war records of States already printed it is hard to say which is the least satisfactory on this point.

The Seven Years' war made the name of Germany and its great leader, Frederick, popular throughout the colonies. Town, village, and wayside inn displayed the well-known sharp features and high shoulders as a sign, and the "King of Prussia" was a favorite name for taverns—then of more importance than to-day—on all the high-roads between the great towns.* Steuben was one of Frederick's own veterans, and as such he was heartily welcomed,

---

* Sauer, the Germantown printer, published in 1761 a translation into German of Dilworth's "Life and Heroic Deeds of Frederick the Great," a volume of 288 pages. Rabbi Franckel's Berlin Thanksgiving Sermon on the King's Victory of December 5, 1757, was reprinted in Philadelphia in 1763, in a translation by an unknown hand (Hildeburn's Issues of the Pennsylvania Press, No. 6725).

when French officers of high rank were coldly received. His zeal, his ability, his success, were shown in the improved discipline and instruction of the provincial troops. He was so good a soldier that he knew just how to use the material at hand, and to make good soldiers and good officers of what had hitherto been an undisciplined mass. Steuben's Regulations long remained the manual of the United States army and its militia. It was not only that he made the army successful in the field, but the discipline he had introduced so effectually cultivated the sense of duty and subordination, that a weak and impotent Congress, which had utterly failed of its duty to provide for its soldiers, was still able to disband peacefully an injured and irritated army. That he spent the rest of his life in waiting for justice is not fairly compensated for by the posthumous honors that have been paid his memory since his death, and the debt of gratitude that America owes to Steuben is one that can never be fully discharged.

Much has been said and written in disparagement of the German mercenaries serving in the British army in the war of independence. It must be borne in mind that in England itself the wickedness of thus hiring men against their consent was sharply denounced. Holland and Russia absolutely refused to accept the tempting offers of Great Britain. King George, himself a German sovereign, mildly protested against thus using his Hanoverian troops. Frederick the Great sternly forbade the enlistment of any of his subjects or permission to any of the petty German princes to take their soldiers through his territories to ports of shipment to England for America. Schiller stigmatized the trade in men in his "Kabale und Liebe," while Kant went still further and embraced the cause of the American colonist with all the energy of his great intellect. Klopstock and Lessing spoke in the same strain, although in lower tones. Frederic Kapp puts the total of twenty-nine thousand one hundred and sixty-six as the number furnished by Brunswick, Hesse-Cassel, Hanau, Waldeck, Anspach, and Anhalt, and of these only seventeen thousand three hundred and thirteen returned to their native country. How many of the remainder stayed in their new home to become fathers of American citizens cannot be easily ascertained, yet it is more than a tradition that in Pennsylvania, in Maryland, in Virginia, in North Carolina, wherever there were German settlers ready to aid the newcomers, the sick, the wounded, the stragglers, the deserters, all found protection and a welcome, which insured them prosperity and a better livelihood than they had left behind them. Their number has been roughly estimated at considerably over ten thousand.

There were many Germans settled in the colonies before the Revolution, who cast their fortunes with the young republic and shared in the struggle which secured independence and union.

The German Battalion was raised agreeably to a resolve of Congress of May 22, 1776, four companies in Pennsylvania and four in Maryland, to which was added a ninth company by resolve of July 9, 1777. The officers were: Lieutenant-Colonel, Ludwick Weltener; Major, Daniel Burckhart; Captains, Jacob Bunner, Peter Boyer, Charles Baltzel, William Rice, Bernard Hubley, Christian Myers, Michael Bayer; Captain-Lieutenant, Philip Schrauder; Lieutenants, John Weidman, Martin Sugart, Jacob Gremeth, Jacob Cramer, Godfrey Swartz, Marcus Young, David Morgan; Ensigns, John Weidman, Henry Shrupp, David Desenderfer, Henry Spech, Jacob Raboldt, Christian Glichner, William Prux, Henry Hehn.

An independent corps of one hundred and fifty

men was raised by resolve of December 5, 1776, of which the officers were: Captains, John Paul Schott, Anthony Selim.

In Henry's account of Arnold's campaign against Quebec, 1775 (Albany, Munsell, 1877), is a reference to the company of riflemen commanded by Captain William Hendricks, from Cumberland County, Pennsylvania, "an excellent body of men, formed by nature as the stamina of an army, fitted for a tough and tight defence of the liberties of their country." Hendricks "was tall, of a mild and beautiful countenance, his soul was animated by a genuine spark of heroism." He was killed at Quebec, in the same attack in which General Montgomery fell, on the 1st of January, 1776, and the two heroes were buried side by side. Provost Smith, in his oration on Montgomery, speaks with unstinted praise of the Pennsylvania riflemen. Their funeral was marked by the British officers with every mark of honor. Of Hendricks's company, raised on the west side of the Susquehanna, scarcely a dozen names have been rescued from oblivion. Of the flower of the country, brave, ardent, and patriotic, and nowise daunted by the sufferings of the Arnold campaign, nearly all of those who returned safely from it served again in the

Revolution. He is spoken of with equal praise by Thayer in his "Journal of the Invasion of Canada in 1775," edited by Stone, published in Providence, Rhode Island, in 1867.

In Harris's "Biographical History of Lancaster County" (Lancaster, 1872), there are many names of its German settlers and their descendants who served as soldiers, with honor to themselves and credit to the race whence they sprang.

In Hamersly's "Dictionary of the Army," and on the register of the army for 1784, there are the familiar names of General Steuben, inspector-general, and his aide-de-camp, Major William North, and that of Major Continental Artillery, Sebastian Bauman, captain New York Continental Artillery Company, 1776, brevet lieutenant-colonel, 1787.

The following hitherto unprinted letter of De Kalb, from the unrivalled collection of Ferdinand J. Dreer, Esq., of Philadelphia, is so characteristic of that hero, in its manly refusal to accept military precedence to Lafayette, that it is well worth publication, as showing the noble nature of the man:

"BETHLEHEM, 18 Septr. 1777.

"SIR,—I have been ever since I had the favour your letter by Mr. Secretary Thomson, in a very uncertain and fluctuating Situation of mind, between the desire of serving in your Army, and the apprehension of blame from home. But Congress and your Esteem do me too much Honour, not to accept your late proposals, if they will grant me Several points I think essential to my tranquillity and entire satisfaction. 1st. That I may be at Liberty to give up my Commission if in answer to the account I will send to France of my proceedings here and my behaviour towards those officers that came over with me, in case they were to exclaim against my stay, in anyway that could be hurtfull to my reputation and honour.

"2nd. As to the offer made to me by the Ministry of Mr. Thomson to have my Commission done of an older date than Marquiss de la Fayette's. I would decline it and have my Commission of the same day with his. That it may be in my power to show my regard for his friendship to me, in giving him the Seniority over me in America, in order, too, not to disgust him.

"3rd. That Congress will be pleased to grant to Chev. Dubuysson, a Commission as Lt. Colonel with only the pay as a Major, or as my aid de Camp.

"4th. That they will please to make provision for

said Chev. Dubuysson of having the assurance of a Pension of 1200 Livres French money or fifty Louis d'ors to be paid in France for life if he serves this and next Campaign, and which they will augment at pleasure if he serves longer and they are satisfied with his having done his duty according to time and circumstances.

"5th. That if Congress are disposed to do anything of that kind for myself it shall be done at their own terms and pleasure. The only thing I could wish in that respect, would be to have the favour bestowed on my Lady and children in case I died in the Continental Army or any other way while in their service.

"On said Conditions I am ready to join the army as soon as possible and to go directly to Philadelphia from Lancaster, where I will wait for a Resolve of Congress, by Chev. Dubuysson, bearer of this.

"Another observation I think necessary in regard to the immediate Command of a Division. General Washington has perhaps friends or deserving officers to whom he would give the preference, in such a case I should be sorry my coming in did in the least cross or prevent his dispositions in this and any other respects. I will gladly and entirely submit to his Commands and to be employed as he shall think most convenient for the good of the Service. If my second aid de Camp I am to chuse, chanced to be a foreigner, I should be glad some provision was made for him after leaving the service, in proportion to his rank as a Major.

"I depend for the Settling of all these matters to the Satisfaction of all parties, on the friendship you are so kind to profess for me, and of which I have already so many proofs. These new obligations cannot increase the respect and high Esteem with which I have the Honour to be,

"Sir,

"Your most obedient,

"Humble Servant,

"BARON DE KALB.

"COLONEL RICHARD HENRY LEE,

"Member of Congress."

This is endorsed:

"Com ^{d} to B ^{d} War

"18th & 23d Sept. 1777, acted upon."

From the same treasure-house of original material for history comes the letter from Steuben, written in French, from which the following is an extract:

"Dear Friend

"I have received your two letters of the 12th and 20th February,—I would rather have seen you in person. I am infinitely obliged to you for your news, for every thing which occurs in the army is of interest. I am infinitely sorry for your account of Col. Bruchs and Major Gils and would be glad to help them. To lose such an officer as Bruchs would be a real misfortune. I have already spoken of it to the President of Congress et je parlerai au bon Dieu et au Diable. I would move Heaven and Earth to prevent it. We are waiting for news from Gibraltar and Charlestown, as the Jews wait for the Messiah. I have bet a hat on the fall of Gibraltar, but I am afraid I shall win only a night cap. Our papers are full of epigrams, abuse, and dreams of the late Mr. de Galvan on the American army,—his friends want to immortalize him. Let me know if North has decided to go beyond Boston, for in that case I fear much,—but no, I won't fear anything. I hoped to present my compliments to Mrs. Washington en route when your last letter reported that she had gone. I would like to see you in my hermitage,—where I am better quartered than since I came to America. I rarely go into the city, but my friends come to see me in my cottage. I receive visits from European Grandees, such as the Prince de Guimené, of the house of Rohan,—who claim to be next after the Bourbons in France. The Duc de Lauzun, the Comte de Gillon, have both been here too. Our American Grandees are too busy with great affairs to pay visits, but I have no pretensions, for I have paid no visit except to the President of Congress, nor will I. Yesterday I was at a supper and ball given by M. de la Luzerne to the newly married Major Moore and his wife,—there were eighty persons, and among them many pretty women. . . . My fate is not yet decided. I have just written to Congress to demand a Committee, to which I can submit my uncomfortable situation. I get no pay, rations or forage, and I live on money I borrow to pay my marketing. My case is one of 'to be or not to be,'—I am ready for anything. The Secretary of War will find it no harder to replace me than the Adjutant-General, whose position he offered to several persons of my acquaintance. 'Let him go' is the favorite phrase of our Secretaries nowadays. I saw Robert Morris yesterday,—he seems more affected by the conditions of the army than anybody. I hope that after the

1st of January, not only will the subsistence of the officers be regularly paid, but that it may be increased. Say to them that no matter what happens, nothing can prevent me from being their advocate. . . . I cannot deal with Lincoln, he has done me more harm than he thinks, but I don't want to be anybody's enemy, not even his. There are some people who are dangerous only as friends, and he is one of them, so it is prudent for me to treat him with indifference. I was not the aggressor, I sought his friendship, and if he had honored me with his confidence, my advice would have been better for him than that of his friend Cornel. . . . The Prince de Guimené wants to make the acquaintance of the General in chief,—he said so to me, and if my finances do not prevent, I will go with him. Although he is only a Midshipman on the Frigate, he is a young man of the highest nobility in France,— a grandson of the Prince de Soubise, who is Marshal of France. I give you warning, so that in case he comes, his air *of a little wild boy* may not prevent you showing him the consideration due to his birth. But what nonsense to talk this way in a Republic. My respects to the General.

"STEUBEN.

"BELISARIUS HALL.
"Nov. the 26th."

The register for 1789 gives, captain First Infantry, David Ziegler (late captain First Pennsylvania Continental Infantry). In the Indian border warfare between 1788 and 1795, a leading figure was that of David Ziegler, whose story is typical of that of many of our early German soldiers. Born in Heidelberg in 1748, he served in the Russian campaign against the Turks under Catharine, until the conquest of the Crimea brought peace. He settled in Lancaster, Pennsylvania, in 1775, and as adjutant of a Pennsylvania regiment, more than half made up of Germans,—the second to enlist under Washington for the war,—and as senior captain of the First Pennsylvania Continental Regiment, he won great praise. Later on he raised a company for war against the Indians in the West, and took part in Clark's expedition, and was with General Harmar in 1790, and with St. Clair in 1791, in command of a battalion of regulars. He was made major and temporarily assigned command of the army, for six weeks, but was led to resign, and was the first mayor of Cincinnati, where he died in 1811. The army list for 1805–6 has, Captain Artillery, Michael Kalteisen, who had been distinguished in connection with the Charleston (South Carolina) German company.

Michael Kalteisen was born at Wachtelsheim, Wurtemberg, on the 18th of June, 1729; in 1762 he was established in business in Charleston, South Carolina, where a large German population had already gathered. In 1766, with fifteen of his countrymen, he established the German Friendly Society of that city, and by the time of the Revolution it counted a hundred members, and was well enough off to advance two thousand pounds to the State for defence against the Crown. On the 12th of July, 1775, he set on foot the plan of a German military organization, which under the name of the German Fusiliers, by 1776, counted over a hundred Germans in its ranks. Its captain was Alexander Gillon, first lieutenant Peter Bouquet (brother of the general of that name), second lieutenant Kalteisen, ensign Gideon Dupont. From the day of their organization they proved themselves true and ardent patriots. In 1779 it took part with the Continental forces under Lincoln and the French squadron under D'Estaing, in the siege of Savannah, having its captain, Scheppert, killed in the same assault in which Pulaski fell. The first captain, Gillon, had been made captain of the South Carolina fleet in 1779, and sent to France to buy three frigates. The

Prince of Luxemburg gave him one for three years, on a guarantee of its safe return and a fourth share of all prize money. He finally led a squadron of eighty sail, and took the "Bahamas." He left a son who, in 1817, was a member of the Fusiliers. Kalteisen died in 1807, and the hall of the German Society, with its tablet in his memory, was destroyed by fire in 1864. The Fusiliers, however, still exist, and the German Society still perpetuates the useful charity set on foot by him.

Of the general officers of the Continental army, the Germans were John De Kalb, F. von de Woedtke, F. W. A. Steuben.

In the pages of that excellent and useful journal, *Der Deutsche Pionier*, the organ of the society established under that name to preserve everything that relates to the history of the German settlers in this country, are found many records of the Germans who served the cause of American liberty, both in the Revolutionary war and in that of the Rebellion. Herkimer in New York, and Muhlenberg in Pennsylvania, are names that will long preserve the memory of the services of the first German soldiers in defence of their adopted country. The records of the Continental army show that in almost every regiment there were Germans, and in those of Pennsylvania, whole regiments, battalions, and companies organized, officered, and filled with Germans, who did good service for their country. In the then western wilderness of Kentucky, Daniel Boone, with others like himself of German birth or descent, did their share in securing American liberty in their new home. In Virginia, North and South Carolina, and Georgia, there were many German settlers, and from their number many went into the patriot army, sharing its hardships and contented with helping to secure the final establishment of American independence as their full reward. In Gustav Körner's "Das Deutsche Element in den Vereinigten Staaten," Cincinnati, 1880, there is a graphic account of the Germans from 1818 to 1848, with frequent reference to the earlier, as well as the later, Germans who took a distinguished place among the soldiers of the young republic in its first Revolution, and in its subsequent wars. Herkimer, Lutterloh, and Weissenfels in New York, Muhlenberg in Pennsylvania, Michael Kalteisen and his associates in the German Fusilier Company of Charleston, South Carolina, the oldest military organization of the country, established in 1775, are among those who were the first German citizens by their sacrifices and their services to secure the right to a place in the home of their adoption.

Friedrich Heinrich Baron von Weissenfels was the friend and companion of Washington, Steuben, and De Kalb, and his name deserves to be rescued from oblivion. Born in Elbing, Prussia, in succession to a line of soldiers (his father was major in the Swedish army), he served in the Silesian war under Frederick the Great, and, like Steuben, won at the hands of that royal soldier his decoration and order; in 1756 he entered the English service to take part in the old French war, was made an officer in the Royal American, the Sixtieth of the line, took part in the attack on Fort Ticonderoga, and the capture of Havana in 1762. He was at the side of Wolfe when he fell at Quebec, and served in the same regiment as St. Clair. Put on half pay at the close of the war, he settled in New York, married a widow Bogart there, and had Steuben and Van Courtland as his groomsmen. As soon as the colonies began the Revolution, casting aside all thought of his own interest, he offered his services to the Continental Congress; was made captain of a regiment organized in New York in 1775, and was brigade-major at

Quebec with Montgomery and Worster. In 1776 he was made lieutenant-colonel in command of the Third Battalion of the Second New York Regiment of the line, and was soon promoted to be colonel, serving at White Plains and at Trenton, and at the capture of Burgoyne, as well as at Monmouth. In 1779 he was second in command under Sullivan in an expedition against the Indians. He was distinguished for his personal gallantry, and was honored by Washington and Congress with many marks of grateful acknowledgment. He died in New Orleans in 1806, poor in purse but rich in glory. His only son died in 1798, in Alexandria, Virginia, his widow in 1818, and his daughter in 1856. He was the first Vice-President of the German Society of New York, with Steuben as its President. He was one of the original members of the Society of the Cincinnati, and his fellow Germans in that organization deserve to be chronicled here, to show the appreciation of their share in the great work of securing the independence of the American republic.

These original members were:

Major-General Steuben, who died in 1795.

Colonel Henry Emanuel Lutterloh, a President of the German Society of New York.

Colonel Nicholas Fish, of New York.

Colonel Frederick von Weissenfels, of the Second New York Regiment.

Major Sebastian Baumann, died 1803, of the Second New York Artillery Regiment.

Captain Henry Ticbout, died 1826, First New York Regiment.

Captain George Sytez, First New York Regiment.

Lieutenant Peter Anspach, Second New York Artillery Regiment.

Lieutenant Henry Demler, Second New York Artillery Regiment.

Lieutenant Joseph Freilich, Second New York Regiment.

Lieutenant Michael Wetzel, Second New York Regiment.

Lieutenant John Furmann, First New York Regiment.

Lieutenant Carl Fr. Weissenfels, Second New York Regiment.

Captain-Lieutenant Peter Neslett, New York Artillery.

Captain-Lieutenant Peter Jaulmann, Sappers and Miners, died 1835.

This list is of the German members of the Society of the Cincinnati in New York alone, and no doubt on the rolls of the Society in other States there will be found many other Germans whose names belong to the roll of soldiers distinguished for their services in the war of the Revolution.

In Seidensticker's admirable and exhaustive "History of the German Society of Pennsylvania," there is a brief mention of the services of the Germans of Philadelphia in the patriot cause. In May, 1776, Congress organized a German regiment, of companies from Pennsylvania and Maryland,—the Pennsylvania companies were five in number, and those from Maryland four. One of the Philadelphia companies was commanded by Colonel David Woelpper, an old soldier, for he had served in Germany under Frederick the Great, and in the old French war under Washington. The German regiment was first commanded by Hausegger, and it served with credit in Muhlenberg's brigade throughout the Revolution. Other German companies were raised at that time, and many Germans served in various arms of the service. The fines and penalties imposed on the German citizens of well-known rebel principles are all recited in Seidensticker's history, showing how strongly the German element in and about Philadelphia adhered to the patriot cause even at the time the British held the city. In Mr. H. M. Jenkins's "History of Gwynedd," there is a similar collection of evidence as to the stout adhesion of the Germans of Montgomery County to the rebel side. He tells the story of one of their number who was charged with the serious offence of giving information to the enemy, and escaped finally severe punishment on the merciful ground that he was a weak politician,—a plea that would cover many offences in our own day and generation.

John Paul Schott, the commander of a battalion in Armand's legion, was born in Prussia in 1744, served as a cadet, became adjutant of Prince Ferdinand of Brunswick, came to America in 1776, was authorized to raise an independent company of German dragoons, led the right wing of Hand's brigade in Sullivan's army, in 1779, in the attack on the Five Nations, and commanded the forts in Wyoming Valley to the close of the war. He filled a variety of civil offices afterwards, dying in Philadelphia in 1829.

Washington's mounted body-guard was led by Major Barth. van Heer, and consisted of fourteen officers and fifty-three men, nearly all Germans. The First Continental Regiment of Pennsylvania was commanded by Colonel John Philipp de Haas, who was born in 1735, came to America in 1750, was ensign in the French war, became a brigadier-general in 1777, took part in the expedition to Canada, and served with credit to the close of the war.

Among the French allied army sent to the help of the struggling colonies were many Germans, and the investigation of H. A. Ratterman, editor of the *Pionier*, attests both their number and influence. It will be found in volume xiii. of that journal (1881), at pages 317, 360, and 420. Colonel Esebeck commanded a regiment, "Zweibrücken" (the German equivalent for the French "Deux Ponts"). In Force's "Archives" many of the details of others are given. At the time it was a matter of arrangement between neighboring and friendly princes, how many of the men of one country should enlist in the army of another. France had troops from the Rhine Provinces, Baden, Bavaria, Würtemberg, Anspach, and Switzerland in its service. With the Zweibrücken Regiment came the two princes of the name, Major Esebeck in command, and Captain Haake. A battalion from Trier served in Custine's regiment, one from Elssass, in the Bourbonnais, a large number were in Lauzun's cavalry regiment, and an Anhalt regiment assisted in the siege of Savannah. Among the German officers in the French service were Count Fersen, chief of staff of Rochambeau, besides his adjutant, Von Closen, and his chief of artillery, Gau. Count von Stedingk commanded the Anhalt regiment, and, like his friend Fersen, belonged to the old Pomeranian nobility, although both afterwards died in the Swedish service.

At Yorktown the Germans in the American army fought for a time against the Germans under the English flag, and the commands were given on both sides in German. A detachment of Germans placed the French flag on the walls of Yorktown after its capture. Among the prisoners were countrymen of the troops put over them as a guard, and many of them met as old friends and neighbors. When Tarleton tried to force his way out of the lines, it was with the German cavalry under Ewald, and they were met and repulsed by the Germans under Armand. Ratterman's estimate that eleven thousand German soldiers remained in this country after the war, may well be credited with recruits from both sides. With the Germans in the Pennsylvania brigade of Muhlenberg and the Maryland brigade of Gist, the soldiers of the German regiments in the English service soon made friends and found new homes. Indeed, the Anspach regiment, two days after the capitulation, offered their services as a body. Elking gives a list of twenty-eight officers of the Brunswick regiment who either remained or returned here after the war to settle.

In the "History of the Early Settlement and Indian Wars of Western Virginia," by Wills de Hass, (Wheeling and Philadelphia, 1851), at page 344, is a brief biographical sketch of Lewis Wetzel, a typical borderer, a brave and successful Indian fighter, and the right arm of the settlers in their almost ceaseless war with the natives. His father was one of the first settlers on Wheeling Creek, and was killed in 1787 by Indians, sacrificing his own life to save that of his comrades. From that time the son, then almost twenty-three years of age, and already well trained by his father, devoted himself to avenging his life. At twenty-five he enlisted under General Harmar, commanding at Marietta, and, while in the army, he shot an Indian, was arrested, escaped, and reached home, in spite of prison, guard, and fetters. An attempt to recapture him was given up out of fear of a counter-rebellion against the United States troops, and when he did get into their hands, General Harmar promptly released him. He went to New Orleans, was there arrested, was released a broken man, yet he was long active in leading new settlers and purchasers through the trackless forests of Western Virginia, until his death in 1808. The name is perpetuated in Wetzel County, West Virginia, although the early German name seems to have passed through numerous variations,—Whetzell, Whitzell, Watzel, and Wetzel,—but of its German derivation there can, of course, be no doubt. The Poes, too, who figure in this border history, were sons of German settlers, from Frederick County, Maryland, and the elder Frederick Poe, who moved west in 1774, and died in 1840 at the age of ninety-three, was, like his younger brother, Andrew, a backwoodsman in every sense of the word. Shrewd, active, and courageous, they fixed their abode on the frontier of civilization, determined to contest inch by inch with the native Indians their right to the soil and their privilege to live. Their hairbreadth escapes and bold adventures remain even now among the legends of their early homes, and fortunately are preserved in the pages of the local historian. As late as 1846 there was found at the mouth of the Kanawha one of the leaden plates suitably inscribed, bearing date 1749, and asserting the claim of France to the region watered by the Ohio River and its tributaries, and others were found at Venango and Marietta. Washington's expedition with the Virginia troops in 1754 first made this region familiar to the colonists, and settlements soon began. From Pennsylvania came some of the German Dunkards, who hoped to practise the peaceful doctrines of their Ephrata brethren, but with them came others more willing to fight than to pray, preferring to take land by force rather than by purchase. Braddock's campaign, with its disaster, only served to make the region better known to the Provincial troops, and from them came the best settlers in the region thus opened. The fate of the Christian and Moravian Indians, settled at Gnadenhütten, Schönbrunn, Salem, and Lichtenau, massacred in cold blood, is a permanent blot upon the leaders in that inexcusable raid, and it was terribly revenged in the utter failure of the next attack, in 1782.

General George Weedon, really Gerhard von der Wieden, was born in Hanover, served in the war of the Austrian Succession, 1742–48, was distinguished for his performance at the battle of Dettingen, served with Colonel Henry Bouquet in Flanders, came with him as lieutenant in his Royal American Regiment, and served with it in the old French war, in the capture of Fort du Quesne, and in the campaign against the Indians. The war over, he settled in Fredericksburg, Virginia, then largely populated by Germans, and when the Revolution broke out became captain and later on lieutenant-colonel of the Third Virginia Militia, colonel of the First Virginia Continental, and finally, on February 24, 1777, brigadier-general, taking a leading part in the battles of Brandywine and Germantown; he left the service for a time, then in 1780 re-entered it under Muhlenberg, and commanded the Virginia militia at the siege of Yorktown.

Armand's legion was originally organized by Nicholas Dietrich Freiherr von Ottendorff, a Saxon nobleman, lieutenant under Frederick the Great, who came to this country with Kosciuszko, and became major, commanding an independent corps of light infantry. It was subsequently reorganized as cavalry under Armand, Ottendorff became lieutenant-colonel, and his adjutant, Howelman, a Hanoverian nobleman, together with the officers of the companies, were all advanced in grade,—the names are given in full in the eighth volume of the *Pionier* (1876-77), p. 436.

Of the Pennsylvania Germans who were soldiers in the Revolution the Hiesters were prominent examples. Four sons of one family were officers: Daniel, the eldest, colonel, John and Gabriel, majors, and William, the youngest, captain; a cousin, Joseph, was in the "Flying Camp," became colonel, later major-general of militia, a member of Congress, and a leader of his party in Berks County down to his death in 1832, in his eightieth year. John and Daniel, too, became major-generals of militia, and they, too, were also sent to Congress, one from Pennsylvania and the other from Maryland, where he made his home.

The knowledge of the early Germans, and their share in our history, will no longer be hidden in the records of scattered local periodicals. In the series of "Geschichtsblätter, Bilder u. Mittheilungen aus dem Leben der Deutschen in Amerika, herausgegeben von Carl Schurz," published in New York by Steiger, we have the promise of a valuable contribution to our slender stock of available information as to the Germans in the United States. The first volume of this series is a reprint of Kapp's "Die Deutschen im Staate New York während des 18ten Jahrhunderts," originally published in Leipsic and New York, in 1867. At page 126 there is a list of the officers of the four battalions organized in Schoharie Valley by Germans, in 1775, to take part in the war of independence. All four colonels were Germans, viz.: Nicholas Herchheimer, First Battalion, Canajoharie; Jacob Kloch, Second Battalion, the Pfalz; Friedrich Fischer, Third Battalion, Mohawk; Hanjost Herchheimer, Fourth Battalion, German Flats. The Herchheimers were the sons of an early German settler in Western New York, who had won distinction by his gallant defence against Indian attacks in the old French war. General Nicholas Herchheimer, who fell in battle in 1777 in defence of the liberties of his country, was honored with the praise of Washington, and by a modest monument which perpetuates his services and sacrifice. One of his soldiers, born in Germany, J. A. Hartmann, survived until 1836, when he died at the age of ninety-two, after an old age of poverty, borne with fortitude, and his name is now best remembered in his old home, where he lived at the public expense, as an example of the tardy gratitude of the republic he too had aided to establish. Herchheimer is the type of the well-to-do settlers of German descent, Hartmann of the poor emigrant, but both did their duty manfully in the struggle for independence, and thus set an example freely followed by others, Germans both by birth and descent, who fought for the Union.

Among the leading German soldiers of the Revolutionary war from New York, was Hermann von Zedwitz, major of the First Regiment; his life is sketched by Alfred Schücking in volume iii., p. 185, of the *Pionier*. The command of Montreal was given to Colonel Rudolph Witzema of the same regiment, an old officer in the Royal Colonial army, who left the Continental army under a cloud, returned to England, and died there in 1803.

The share of the Germans as officers and soldiers on the patriot side in the war of the Revolution won them the confidence and gratitude of Washington. The Hessians under Riedesel, who surrendered with Burgoyne, were sent to Virginia, where they lived near Jefferson, who thus learned to know them, gave them the use of his library, and enjoyed their music.

The second volume of Schurz's series, "Bilder aus der Deutsch Pennsylvanischen Geschichte," is from the pen of Professor Oswald Seidensticker, whose services in the cause of our local German history have received general acknowledgment for their thoroughness and accuracy. He describes in detail the part taken by the Germans of Pennsylvania in both the Continental army under Washington and the Provincial or State militia, and gives the names of the officers of the German Battalion, and their share in the war of independence. In the Second, Third, Fifth, Sixth, and Eighth Pennsylvania Regiments were many Germans. The Second was commanded by Colonel Philippe de Haas; the lieutenant-colonel of the Third was Robert Bunner, who fell at Monmouth, in 1778; and Mentges of the Fifth and Becker of the Sixth were also Germans. Many of these were members of the German Society, and Colonel Farmer, first captain of a company of sharpshooters, and later commissary-general, was four times president of the German Society after the war.

Reading sent three Hiesters, and York many Germans, in the regiments that served in the Revolution. Pennsylvania Germans were numerous in Armand's legion, in Schott's dragoons, and in Van Heer's cavalry brigade. Quakers, Mennonites, Dunkers, and Herrnhüters sacrificed their religious tenets and associations to serve their country, while the Lutherans and others who had no conscientious scruples against bearing arms, were well represented in the field. Foremost among these was General Muhlenberg, born in Montgomery County in 1746, the son of the oldest clergyman of the Lutheran Church in Pennsylvania, who destined all his three sons to follow him in the church, educated at Halle, settled in 1772 in Virginia, as pastor of a German Lutheran congregation in the Shenandoah Valley. He there became a friend of Patrick Henry and Washington. Earnestly supporting the cause of American independence, he became colonel of the Eighth Virginia, with Abraham Bowman and Peter Helfenstein as his field-officers. In January, 1776, he preached his last sermon, urging on his hearers the duty of patriotic devotion to the cause of the country, and then, throwing aside the clerical gown, showed his military uniform, and instantly over three hundred of his listeners followed his example and joined his regiment. Congress soon made him a brigadier-general, and throughout the war his zeal, his courage, his energy, were appreciated by Washington and Lafayette, and the other leaders of the Revolution. His part in the final surrender of Cornwallis at Yorktown made him a major-general, and yet so modest was he that when peace returned his old parishioners would gladly have made him once more their pastor. Seven years of war had, however, changed the current of his thoughts, and settling in Philadelphia, he became vice-president of the State, under Franklin, and, owing to Franklin's age and infirmities, was practically the head of the government. In 1788 he and his brother worked energetically to secure the adoption of the Constitution of 1789, and under it he sat in the First Congress, as well as in the Second and the Sixth, always a stout advocate of the Democratic party; he was three times president of the German Society. His descendants, and those of his venerable father, have served the state and the church in many ways, and always with honor to their German blood. His statue stands in the Capitol at Washington, as the representative man chosen by Pennsylvania to take a place among the heroes gathered there from all parts of the country. His name and his fame are part of the inheritance which the German population of Pennsylvania transmits to future generations to show how thoroughly the German element has done its duty alike in war and in peace, and how well it deserves to have its record preserved and published for the information of their descendants and of the country.

Many of the early settlers of Kentucky were Germans from Virginia and North Carolina, and they held the frontier outposts against the incursions of hostile Indians. Many old Revolutionary soldiers there found homes, and their sons were active in the war of 1812. Frankfort, the capital of the State, owes its name to its German founders, for the most part emigrants from Frankfort-on-the-Main, and its vicinity, who came hither in 1786–87. The first physician was Dr. Louis Marschall, father of Humphrey Marshall, noted in both the civil and military history of Kentucky. Thus many of the German names were anglicized, some—*e.g.*, Jäger translated into Hunter—completely disguised, yet the industry of local historians has shown that a very large part of the early settlement of Kentucky was made by Germans.

Among the soldiers of German descent a marked and exceptional case is that of General John A. Quitman. He was the son of the pastor of the German Lutheran Church of Schoharie, who was himself born in Iserlohn, Germany, and came to this country in 1795. The father was a strong, determined man, with a high notion of his own importance, who showed a will of his own not unlike that of the son. The elder Quitman left Schoharie to become pastor of the church in Rheinbeck, where he died in 1832. His son was born there in 1798, and educated by his father's successor. As a young man he went South, became a distinguished lawyer and member of Congress from his new home in Natchez, Mississippi, took a leading place among the general officers of volunteers in the Mexican war, was prominent in urging on the people of the South the extreme doctrines of States' rights, rejoicing in the name of fire-eater, and was generally looked on as the intellectual leader of the agitation which finally ended in the Rebellion of 1861. His death, in 1858, saved him from sharing in the devastation his theories had brought over the section which accepted him as their representative.

In the Revolution there were adherents of Whigs and Tories even in the same family, and this was as true of the Germans as of the other nationalities settled in the colonies; but in the Rebellion the minority in either of the two great sections into which the country was divided had little power or influence to stem the tide that finally led to the success of the Union. Still, the Germans were found on both sides, for the self-reliant, independent character of the German leads him to choose his own course, and to adhere to it in spite of popular opposition. In Arkansas, Klingelhöffer, son of the founder of a German colony at Little Rock, became an officer of the Confederate army.

The registers and rolls of the regular army of the United States bear the names of many distinguished soldiers of German birth and descent, and not a few of them brought to the service of their new fatherland the training and experience acquired in their native country. In the exhaustive dictionaries of the army by Gardiner and Henry and Hamersly, and in the invaluable pages of General George W. Cullum's "Record of the Graduates of West Point," are found many examples of the German soldier in the army of the United States. One example deserves special mention.

John Baptiste de Barth, Baron de Walbach, brigadier-general and colonel commanding Fourth Artillery, U.S.A., was the third son of Count Joseph de Barth and Marie Therese de Rohmer. He was born in Munster, Valley of St. Gregory, Upper

Rhine, Germany, on the 3d day of October, 1766, and was educated at the military school at Strasbourg. In December, 1792, he entered as a cadet the company commanded by Baron de Wald, Regiment of Royal Alsace, Prince Maximillian of Deux Ponts colonel and proprietor, in the service of the King of France. He was promoted and served in the same regiment as ensign until October, 1783, and then until November as gentleman volunteer in the hussars, General Baron de Kellerman commanding. From January, 1783, until January 9, 1784, he served in the Regiment of Luzern Hussars, when he received the appointment of sub-lieutenant (cornet), and continued to serve in the successive grades, second lieutenant, first lieutenant, until May, 1792, and captain. Declining the commission of captain, he left France to join the armies of the Prince, brother of King Louis XVI. He served in this army as gentleman volunteer, on horseback, at his own expense, under Colonel Count de Pestalozzi, his former colonel of the Luzern Hussars. With this corps he made the campaign in Champagne, in 1792, in the advance of the Prussian army, until it was disbanded at Maestrich. He then left Liege, passed through the French lines to Treves, and brought back his sister, Mme. Blondeau, and placed her, with their three children, under the care of her husband, lieutenant-colonel, formerly major, of artillery, who had served in the army of Rochambeau in America. He then went to Germany, took part in the attack on Frankfort, January 6, 1793, and later joined the Sixty-second Company, First Battalion of the Austrian Chasseurs of Condé, serving, during the campaign of 1793, in attacks on the French lines at Germersheim, Yorkheim, Langenkardet, and Weissembourg, where the Austrians captured one hundred and fifty-five pieces of cannon; the losses in both armies being estimated at twenty-two thousand men. He then accepted a captaincy from the Prince de Rohan, and covered the retreat of the unfortunate army of the Duke of York northward to Holland and Germany. Finally he embarked with his regiment, the Hussars of Rohan, for the British West Indies, on the promise of the British Government that they should always serve on horseback, and that at the end of four years they were to be returned to their homes. In 1798, being then the third officer of the regiment, which had been reduced by yellow fever from twelve hundred to one hundred and thirty, he obtained leave for six months to visit his father, who had come to America at the outbreak of the French Revolution. With twenty-four other noblemen he had agreed to buy forty thousand acres of land on the Scioto River, Ohio, paying half the purchase-money to Joel Barlow and William Playfair, agents in Paris of Colonel William Duer, accredited by a letter from Thomas Jefferson. Count de Barth sailed with three hundred emigrants, landed in Alexandria, Virginia, in March, 1790, and then proceeded to Marietta, Ohio, where he found that Duer had become a bankrupt. He returned to Philadelphia, purchased a country-seat,—Springettsbury Manor, Bush Hill, a mansion with sixty acres,—but he died there September 24, 1793, and was buried in St. Mary's Roman Catholic Church in Philadelphia. Bush Hill was occupied as a hospital during the yellow fever, and as there was no one authorized to make the last payment, it was sold by the sheriff and passed from the family. In 1798 Colonel, then Major, Walbach, on his arrival, retained Messrs. William Rawle, Jared Ingersoll, and James Heatly, but owing to the loss of documents could obtain no redress. Major Walbach then resigned his commission as major in the Hussars of Rohan and became an adopted citizen of the United States. In the autumn of 1798 he entered the army of the United States on the invitation of Washington, Hamilton, and McHenry, as second lieutenant of cavalry, and was appointed adjutant of a cavalry regiment, holding that post until the corps was disbanded in June, 1799. He then was employed in the office of the Adjutant-General of the United States, General William North, who had been aid to General Steuben. In December, 1799, he was employed to assist General Charles C. Pinckney in preparing regulations for the cavalry, and later to assist General Hamilton in preparing regulations for the artillery, and afterwards he was ordered to report to General Washington, to take charge of a detachment of dragoons. He was appointed, in 1801, first lieutenant in the First Regiment of Artillery and Engineers, and in 1802 aid to General Wilkinson; in 1804, adjutant of artillery and military agent at Fort Constitution, New Hampshire; in 1806, captain of artillery; in 1812, assistant deputy quartermaster; in 1813, assistant adjutant-general with the rank of major, and assistant adjutant-general with the rank of colonel, and brevet major, for gallant conduct at the battle of Chrystler's Fields;

in 1815, major of artillery and brevet lieutenant-colonel; in 1830, brevet colonel for ten years' further service, and lieutenant-colonel in the First Regiment of Artillery; in 1842, colonel of the Fourth Regiment of Artillery, and made commander at Fortress Monroe and brevet brigadier-general; and in 1851 he was assigned to the command of the Department of the East. He died in Baltimore, Maryland, on the 10th of June, 1857, of disease contracted in the war of 1812. A highly commendatory order was issued by General Scott, lieutenant-general commanding at the time of his death, reciting his long military career, his distinguished services, and his unwavering integrity, truth, and honor, strict attention to duty, and zeal for the service, tempering the administration of an exact discipline by the most elevated courtesies. General George W. Cullum, in his "Campaigns and Engineers of the War of 1812–15," at page 168, credits him with saving the artillery at Chrystler's Fields in 1813. His grandson, John de Barth Walbach Gardiner, is an assistant surgeon in the United States army. His son, L. de B. Walbach, who died in 1853, was a graduate of West Point and a captain of ordnance. Another son died an officer of the United States navy.

General Walbach is well remembered by old officers of the regular army as a fine soldierly character, full of zeal and pride in his profession, and a man of many manly virtues and attractive qualities. His brother was a Roman Catholic priest in Baltimore, and in their old age these two men, living together, were typical examples of the professions of war and peace.*

Among the early graduates of West Point, a notable example of the way in which Germany has supplied our army with officers is the case of Julius F. Heileman, son of the surgeon of Riedesel's German Brigade in Burgoyne's army; he was appointed a cadet in 1803, and rose to be major of the Second Artillery, when he fell in Florida, in 1836.

George Nauman was a graduate of West Point in 1823, who rose by slow but good service, and died as lieutenant-colonel of the First Artillery in Philadelphia in 1863. He was born in Pennsylvania sixty years before.

---

* The battle of Leipsic, the turning-point of the uprising of Germany against Napoleon, was celebrated in Philadelphia by German citizens, with toasts in honor of the Emperor of Russia, the burning of Moscow, Blücher, the German Princes, and the Patriots of South America.

General Ammen, who was distinguished during the Rebellion, was a native of Virginia, a graduate of West Point in 1831, had resigned to engage in teaching and engineering, and, when the war broke out, re-entered the service as colonel of the Twenty-fourth Ohio; as a brigadier-general, he served with great bravery in the West.

Edmund Schriver and Alexander Shiras were graduates of 1833, and both were born in Pennsylvania. Their services in the Rebellion were highly appreciated.

Herman Haupt, a graduate of 1835, was born in Philadelphia, and, besides his services in the field, has been a pioneer in the great business of railroad building across the continent. His son graduated in 1867.

Luther and Roland and Hagner, all of the class of 1836, bore good Pennsylvania German names.

The Muhlenbergs have had a representative, and often more than one, in the regular army since the time of the early Pennsylvania soldier down to our own day, and all have done honor to a name that is looked on as one fittingly chosen as the type of the Pennsylvania soldier and statesman. The Muhlenbergs, six at least, fill an honored place on the registers of the regular army, in which they have a right by descent from patriot ancestors of the Revolution.

General S. P. Heintzelman, a veteran of the regular army, was born in Lancaster County in 1805. His grandfather, a native of Augsburg, was the first white settler in Manheim, where his grandson was educated until he went to West Point in 1826. He was promoted and brevetted for his gallantry in the Mexican war, and at the outbreak of the Rebellion became colonel of the Seventeenth United States Infantry. At Bull Run he was wounded; on the Peninsula he commanded a corps, and throughout the war he was always on duty.

Francis Lieber was born in Berlin in 1800; he grew up in the midst of the earnest aspirations of Germany for freedom from the French yoke, and at the age of fifteen, following the example of his elder brothers, and with the approval of his parents, enlisted in the Colberg Regiment under Blücher. He began his short experience of war at Ligny, was wounded, and returned after the campaign of Waterloo to resume his work as a school-boy. With the other young Turners, he followed Jahn in his plan for political as well as physical regeneration, and with his leader he was imprisoned for excess of patriotism.

His four months' confinement was not in itself a great hardship, but it carried with it a prohibition to study in any Prussian university, and this implied his exclusion from public employment. He studied at Jena, Halle, and Dresden, and then at twenty-one took part in the Greek struggle, with very unsatisfactory results.

Then, encouraged by Niebuhr, in whose family he had been employed in Rome, he returned to Berlin, only to be again imprisoned, an enforced idleness which he used in the composition of a volume of poems of the merriest kind; after trying in vain to secure a stable position, he freed himself from the uncomfortable results of his early patriotism by coming to America, where he arrived in 1827. He established a swimming-school in Boston after the model of those of Germany, but soon undertook a very great work,—the preparation of the "Encyclopædia Americana," based on Brockhaus's "Conversations Lexicon," published in Philadelphia, which then became the scene of his active literary labors. He prepared an elaborate scheme for the management of Girard College, and began his independent authorship. He went to the University of South Carolina, in 1835, as Professor of History and Political Economy. There he wrote and taught until 1857, when he gladly left the South.

When the Rebellion broke out he was quietly settled at Columbia College in New York, but one of his sons went into the Confederate service, another with the Illinois troops into the Union army, and a third got a commission in the regular army, and he himself began his work as legal adviser to the government on questions of military and international law by preparing a code of instructions for the government of armies of the United States in the field, and from that time on he was in constant employment in that direction, putting his vast store of learning at the disposition of the authorities on every fitting occasion. He maintained a close correspondence with the leading German professors Bluntschli, Mohl, Holtzendorff, and did much to secure in Germany a proper appreciation of the great work done for the world by securing the perpetuation of the American Union, and later on to make America alive to the merits of the great struggle with France which secured German unity. His busy life ended in 1872, and his best epitaph was his own favorite motto, "Patria Cara, Carior Libertas, Veritas Carissima," for Country, Liberty, and Truth, were the great aims in all he wrote and spoke and thought. His services were of a kind not often within the reach and range of a single life, and his memory deserves to be honored and kept green in both his native and his adopted country. He was well represented in the Union cause by his two sons, Hamilton, who served in the Ninety-second Illinois, and died in 1876, an officer of the regular army, and Guido, still in the regular service, through whom his name is perpetuated in the army register, while the death of another son on the Confederate side was another sacrifice to the cause of the Union.

His "Instructions for Armies in the Field," General Order No. 100, published by the Government of the United States, April 24, 1863, were the first codification of international articles of war, and marked an epoch in the history of international law and of civilization. His other contributions to military and to international law, published at various times during the civil war, together with his other miscellaneous writings on political science, have been reprinted in the two volumes of his works issued by J. B. Lippincott & Co., in 1881, and these, with his memoirs and the tributes paid him by President Gilman and Judge Thayer, are his best monument. A memoir by T. S.

Perry well deserves attention, and the German translation, edited by Holtzendorff, shows Lieber's popularity in Germany.

General August V. Kautz was born in Baden in 1828, and came as a lad to this country, where his family settled in Ohio. At the outbreak of the Mexican war he enlisted in the First Ohio Regiment, and was rewarded for his services by being appointed a lieutenant in the regular army. He was captain of cavalry at the outbreak of the Rebellion, commanded his regiment, the Sixth Cavalry, under McClellan, in the operations before Richmond, was appointed colonel of the Second Ohio Cavalry and chief of cavalry of the Twenty-third Corps, and brevetted major-general in both the volunteer and regular service. He became lieutenant-colonel of the Fifteenth Infantry after the war, is now colonel of the Eighth Infantry, and is the author of some excellent works on various subjects of military science.

Brevet Lieutenant-Colonel Alfred Mordecai, of the Ordnance Department of the United States army, is a graduate of West Point, of the class of June, 1861, and is now major of his corps. His scientific services have been recognized both in and out of the army. He is the son of a distinguished officer of the regular army, Major A. Mordecai, of the class of 1823, whose military record was a very brilliant one; his name is familiar as the author, with General McClellan and General Delafield, of an admirable report of their visit to Europe and to the Crimea during the Russian war of 1854. His grandfather was a German. Father and son have both contributed to the science of their branch of the military profession, ordnance; and the elder, Major Mordecai, gave the first impulse to Professor Henry's application of electricity to ballistics,— the art of measuring the velocity of projectiles, now become a matter of every-day use in all arsenals throughout the world.

General George A. Custer, one of the most picturesque characters of the war and an exceptional soldier in his Indian campaigns, was the great-grandson of an officer of the Hessian soldiers sent here to serve in the British army during the Revolution. His ancestor, paroled in 1778, after Burgoyne's surrender, settled in Pennsylvania, married there, changed his German name, "Küster," to one easier to pronounce in English, and moved to Maryland, where the father of General Custer was born in 1806. His famous son was born in Ohio, in 1839, as a boy taught school in his native village, Hopedale, until 1857, when he was appointed a cadet at West Point. Graduating there in June, 1861, he was assigned to the Second Cavalry, served with distinction, was made a captain on the staff of General McClellan, served with General Kearney and General Pleasonton, was appointed a brigadier-general for his gallantry at the battle of Aldie, and commanded, successively, a brigade and a division of cavalry, which he led with distinguished bravery. He was promoted to be a major-general of volunteers, a brevet major-general of the United States army, and lieutenant-colonel of the Seventh Cavalry, served under General Hancock in a series of campaigns against the Indians, and finally fell in battle with the Sioux. He was the author of many capital contributions to the periodical literature after the civil war, and his memory is preserved in his wife's charming little book, "Military Life on the Frontiers," and in the "Life of General Custer," by F. Whittaker, published shortly after his heroic death in June, 1876.

Lieutenant John T. Greble, of the Second Artillery, a graduate of West Point, of the class of

1854, is well remembered as the first officer of the regular army to fall in the war of the Rebellion. Born in Philadelphia in 1834, he was killed in action, at Big Bethel, Virginia, on the 10th of June, 1861. He was one of the most popular officers in the service, distinguished alike for gallantry and attainments. He, too, was of German descent, and the traditions of the family were all patriotic. His great-grandfather, Andrew Greble, a native of Saxe-Gotha, came to this country in 1742, settled permanently in Philadelphia, and enlisted warmly in the cause of the war of Independence. He and his four sons joined the American army, and fought at the battles of Princeton and Monmouth. Two of his ancestors on his mother's side, good Welsh Quakers, were in the Continental army. A graduate of the Philadelphia High School, he showed at West Point and in the army a love of study, which, with his amiable manners and soldierly conduct, secured him the friendship of all with whom he was brought in contact. After serving in Florida, he was appointed to the corps of instructors at West Point, and was on duty at Fortress Monroe when the civil war broke out. His untimely death was due to his deliberate purpose to sacrifice his life to save the lives of the large body of soldiers imperilled by an overwhelming force. His heroism had its reward in the gratitude with which his memory is cherished both in the army and by the people. His son, Lieutenant Edwin St. John Greble, a graduate of the class of 1881, is now serving with the Second United States Artillery.

William Heine was born in 1827, died in Dresden, his native city, in October, 1885. He learned landscape and architectural painting in Paris, and was employed as a painter at the Dresden Court Theatre, but, after the revolution of 1848 in Saxony, came to the United States in 1851; he travelled in Central America, which he described in "Wanderbilder aus Centralamerika," Leipzig, 1853. He subsequently joined Perry's expedition to Japan, and, in 1860, the Prussian expedition to the same country, describing it in his "Japan, Beiträge zur Kentniss des Landes u.s. Bewohner," Dresden, 1870. After the outbreak of the American civil war, he entered the Union army as captain of engineers; advanced to the rank of brigadier, March, 1865; was afterwards employed in the United States consular service, and returned to his native land in 1871.

The Germans served in large numbers in cavalry and artillery companies of volunteers in the Mexican war, notably from Texas and Missouri, and many of them gained distinction in this service. Kentucky had its infantry regiment and its cavalry company of Germans in the Mexican war, and many Germans in its loyal regiments during the Rebellion, notably Companies E and G of the Fourth Cavalry, and Barth's company of the Twenty-eighth Kentucky Volunteers. Among the Germans whose services in Texas ought not to be forgotten is the once familiar name of William Langenheim; and of his associates, Gustavus Schleicher in Texas and J. A. Wagener in South Carolina served in the Confederate army. New Orleans and Louisiana had among their leading Union men two representative Germans,—Christian Roselius and Michael Hahn.

General Godfrey Weitzel was born in Germany in 1835, and came with his parents to this country as a child, was appointed a cadet at West Point in his seventeenth year, and in 1855 graduated as a lieutenant of engineers. He served with Butler and Banks in the South, and led a division under Grant in the final conquest of Richmond. After the war he was constantly employed in his profession, until his untimely death in Philadelphia, March 19, 1884.

Colonel Alexander von Schrader, born in Germany, a soldier by training, was lieutenant-colonel of the Seventy-fourth Ohio, and became a major in the Thirty-ninth Infantry of the regular army, dying in service August 6, 1867. He had been reduced to the direst poverty before the war, but when the occasion came his distinguished gallantry and efficient military training stood him in good stead.

Henry A. Hambright, retired as major Nineteenth United States Infantry, brevet colonel United States army, brevet brigadier-general United States volunteers, was born in Lancaster, Pennsylvania, March 24, 1819. His father, Frederick, a major-general of militia, and his uncle, George, a colonel, both served in the war of 1812. Colonel Hambright served in the Mexican war, in the war of the Rebellion as an officer of the Second Pennsylvania Volunteers, in the First Pennsylvania (three months) Volunteers, and as colonel of the Seventy-ninth Pennsylvania; while still in the three months' service he was commissioned captain of the Eleventh United States Infantry, and served with distinguished gallantry through the war, and with great fidelity until he was retired for disability incurred in the line of duty.

A study of the register of officers of the regular army from 1779 shows a large proportion of Germans,—beginning with Kalb and Steuben, in the German Battalion of Pennsylvania and Maryland, the artillery and engineer and other staff corps engaged in the wars of 1812 and 1846. During the Rebellion many old soldiers of German birth were rewarded by commissions, and not a few distinguished German volunteers were also appointed in the regular army,—among them Blücher, Von Hermann, Luettwitz, Michalowski, Von Schirach.

There were two million six hundred and ninety thousand men engaged in the army and navy during the Rebellion, beside seventy-two thousand emergency men called out for short periods of service. The Count of Paris, in his exhaustive history of the war, says that of the volunteers who enlisted during the first year only one-tenth were foreigners; of the remainder, two-thirds were born on American soil and less than one-fourth were naturalized Europeans. In 1864, when conscription was partially resorted to, eighty per cent. were natives. This army, more than two-thirds natives and less than one-third foreigners, was raised out of a population of nineteen millions. Far more than one-third of the effective male population were of European birth, yet in the army there was less than that proportion in the ranks.

The Confederacy at the time of the battle of Bull Run had about two hundred thousand men under arms. When the North called for five hundred thousand men, the South called for four hundred thousand. In 1862 the South had about one hundred and eighty thousand men in the field; in April of that year the Confederate Congress ordered, not a draft as in the past, but a levy *en masse* of all white males between eighteen and thirty-five, residing within the Confederacy, for three years or the war, divided into sixteen classes. Based on a population of five million whites, this should have produced eight hundred thousand men,—it did give between four and five hundred thousand effective men. In September, 1862, the limit of age was extended to forty-five, and the other limit was made to include all who had completed their seventeenth year since April.

In the Confederate army there were many Germans, and much of the literature of the war on the part of the South is made up of the records of those who served on that side,—notable among them Heros von Borcke, and he speaks in his Munchausen-like book of finding among the riflemen an old Prussian soldier from Texas,—of meeting at Lee's headquarters Captain Scheibert, of the Prussian engineers, detailed as an observer, but taking an active part as a combatant,—and the author of a book, "Sieben Monate in den Rebellen Staaten," published in Stettin in 1868, characterized by its strong Southern tone.* Then there is the book of another German

---

* In McClellan's admirable life of General J. E. B. Stuart, there is a paper signed by that distinguished officer under date of June 17, 1862, in which he says,—

"M. Heros von Borcke, a Prussian cavalry officer, has shown himself a thorough soldier and a splendid officer. I hope the [War] Department will confer as high a commission as possible on this deserving man, who has cast in his lot with us in this trying hour." (p. 69.)

At page 307, we find that on the 19th of August, 1863, Major Heros von Borcke, an officer of the Prussian army, who was serving on General Stuart's staff, received a severe wound, which disabled him from further service. (p. 307.)

In the Southern Bivouac Magazine, for February, 1886, published at Louisville, Kentucky, it is mentioned at page 515 that the distinguished Colonel Von Borcke, Stuart's chief-of-staff, lately revisited Fauquier County, Virginia, staying near Upperville, on the northern border; his once robust constitution much affected by the ball he soldier of fortune, B. Estvan, whose "Kriegsbilder aus Amerika" appeared in Leipsic in 1864, as it had already been published in England and in New York in English in 1863. Fritz Annecke, a soldier in the West, published a work on " Der zweite Freiheitskrieg," in Frankfort in 1861,—H. Blankenburg another coming down to the Presidential election in 1868 (Leipsic, 1869); August Conrad " Schat-

---

still carries in his right lung, received when he was wounded in 1863; but his jovial, impulsive, warm-hearted nature has not forsaken him. Colonel von Borcke served on the staff of Prince Frederic Charles, in the war of 1866, but his old wounds forced him to retire.

Captain Scheibert's interest in the Southern cause did not end with the war; on returning to Germany, where he became major in the Prussian Engineers, he corresponded with the editor of the Southern Historical Society's Papers. In vol. v., p. 90, his letter on Gettysburg, dated Stuttgart, November 21, 1879, is printed, and in vol. iv., p. 88, there is a notice by Colonel Venables, C.S.A., of a translation of Scheibert's book into French, by Captain Bonnecque, of the French Engineers. In 1883, Major Scheibert published a German translation of Allan's " History of the Valley Campaign ;" and in a letter of October 13, 1881, dated at Hirshberg, Silesia, Prussia, he says he has translated and printed in German, Early's " Gettysburg," Stuart's and Lee's " Reports," Hubbard's " Chancellorsville," Patton's "Jackson," McClellan's " Jeb Stuart," Stuart's " Gettysburg," and biographies of Lee, Jackson, Stuart, and Mosby. His " Burgerkrieg in den Vereinigten Staaten" has been translated into French and Spanish.

ten und Lichtbilder aus dem amerikanischen Leben wahrend des Secessionskrieges" (Hannover, 1879); Rüstow, a recognized authority on war, a history of the war, from a purely military point of view. Mangold wrote "Der Feldzug in Neu Virginien in August, 1862" (Hannover, 1881), which has received high praise,—Constantin Sander, a history of the war, first down to 1862, and then a later and more complete volume, the former published in Frankfort in 1863, the second in 1865. "Von Achten der Letzte" is a German novel on the Southern side published in Wiesbaden in 1871. Much that is of interest on the subject is to be found in the volume, "In der neuen Heimath, Geschichtliche Mittheilungen über die Deutschen Einwanderer in allen Theilen der Union, herausgegeben von Anton Eickhoff." 2te Ausgabe, N. Y., Steiger, 1885, 8vo, pp. 398.

Of translations and newspaper magazine articles in German, the number is almost endless. Many Southern citizens living abroad tried to reach the German public by arguments and appeals, but the fact remains that the great mass of the German people were from first to last unshaken in their faith in the success of the Union, and they profited largely by the faith which led them to make investments in American bonds and securities at a time of general doubt.

In North Carolina there was a goodly number of Germans and of the descendants of the early German settlers in the Confederate service. In Wilmington, North Carolina, at the commencement of the war, a company was raised under the name of the German Volunteers, afterwards Company A, Eighteenth Regiment North Carolina troops. The officers were, C. Cornehlsen, Captain; H. Vollers, First Lieutenant; G. H. W. Runge, Second Lieutenant; E. Schulken, Third Lieutenant. There were seventy-five men rank and file, all Germans, in this organization, while in other branches of the service, artillery and cavalry, as well as in the Confederate States navy, there were Germans,—so that North Carolina had a fair share of them in its volunteers.

South Carolina was not without its German soldiers. Indeed, as early as 1670, the first German that set foot in Carolina, John Lederer, made a tour of exploration under the direction of Governor William Berkeley, of Virginia; he was a man of learning; his journal was written in Latin, and the translator, Sir William Talbot, Governor of Maryland, speaks highly of his literary attainments. The account of this journey was published and circulated, and doubtless had its effect in the settling of Carolina, for it is certain that in 1680 German immigration had fairly set in. In 1764 six hundred Palatines arrived in South Carolina. In 1766 the German Friendly Society was founded in Charleston, and as early as 1686 the German Lutherans were included among the leading elements of the population. Between 1730 and 1750 a great addition was made from Switzerland and Germany, and the dreadful war that scourged the peaceful inhabitants for so many years drove thousands to America, and of these many came to Carolina. Of course in the Confederacy, and especially in its army from South Carolina and in the defence of Charleston, there were many Germans; thus in the force that took possession of Fort Moultrie in April, 1861, there was the German Artillery, Captain C. Nohrden; and among the troops furnished by the city of Charleston to the Southern army, in the roster printed in Courtenay's History of Charleston, are the following German organizations, viz.:

Fourth Brigade South Carolina Militia: German Riflemen, Captain J. Small; Palmetto Riflemen, Captain A. Melchers.

Seventeenth Infantry, German Fusileers, Captain S. Lord, Jr.

First Regiment of Artillery, Major John A. Wagener (a veteran of the war with Mexico, a member of Company F, the Charleston company of the South Carolina Regiment).

German Artillery, Company A, Captain C. Nohrden; German Artillery, Company B, Captain H. Harms.

Cavalry, German Hussars, Captain Theodore Cordes.

Marion Rifles, a volunteer corps of the fire department, Captain C. B. Sigwald.

At the commencement of the war of the Rebellion, the Germans of Charleston, South Carolina, took an active share in the war, for they considered that their homes were assailed by the North, and they volunteered freely for the war, furnishing about four hundred men. The German Artillery, Companies A and B, were militia organizations, under command of Major John A. Wagener. These two companies served from the outset until the war ended. The two companies were under the respective command of Captains A. Nohrden and H. Harms. After the battle of Hilton Head, November 7, 1861, Major

Wagener took command of the Home Guards in Charleston, and the commander of Company A was Captain D. Werner; of Company B, Captain Franz Melchers, who served during the rest of the war. The command was reorganized after the war as one company, under Captain F. W. Wagener, who had served during the war after Captain Werner's resignation. The German Hussars, also a militia company, volunteered for the war under Captain Theodore Cordes; on his death, Captain Fremder took command, and after his death, Captain Hanke Wohlken served during the war. The German Volunteers were a company of young men under Captain W. K. Bachman; they volunteered for and served throughout the war. All of them declared their allegiance to the home they had chosen voluntarily and shared the fate of the people who had received them kindly, while they hardly bothered their heads about the cause of the war. They were merchants, clerks, artisans, etc., and many of them have passed away during or since the war. Captain F. Melchers still survives,—for forty years a resident of Charleston, and for thirty-three years publisher of the *Deutsche Zeitung*, except during the four years of the war, when he served as lieutenant and as captain, and as lieutenant-colonel on the staff of General Wade Hampton. Captain F. W. Wagener and Captain Hanke Wohlken are merchants, Captain W. R. Bachman a lawyer, and Professor C. H. Bergmann, of the German School, was a volunteer and orderly sergeant in Bachman's company during the war. The survivors are about to erect a monument to their fallen comrades, and the Germans of Charleston have contributed a handsome sum for the purpose.

The Charleston companies in the armies of the Confederate States for the war (1861–65) included in Courtenay's roster:

Three companies of German artillery.

Light Battery B,* Hampton Legion, Captain W. K. Bachman.

Light Battery A, Captain F. W. Wagener.

Light Battery B, Captain F. Melchers.

Marion Rifles, Company A, Twenty-fourth Regiment South Carolina Volunteers, Captain C. B. Sigwald.

---

* This company, called the German Volunteers, was raised by the German citizens of Charleston, mustered into service for the war as an infantry company, and subsequently transferred to the light artillery.

German Hussars, Troop G, Third Regiment South Carolina Cavalry, Captain Theodore Cordes.

In Texas many Germans served in the Confederate army. In Walker's Texas Division, the Third Texas Volunteer Infantry Regiment had Company B, Captain Biesenbuch, Lieutenants Koening and Uhl; Company F, Captain Rosenheimer, Lieutenants Ztuni and Hafner; Company G, Captain Sherhagen; Company K, Captain Bosi, Lieutenants Sarasin and Schleuning. In the Sixteenth Texas, Colonel Flournoy, Company E, Captain G. T. Marold, Lieutenants Klaedon, Hanke, and Groff; Company H, of the Seventeenth, Captain Sabath, Lieutenant Kollmauer, were all Germans.

In the First Virginia Infantry, Company K had Lieutenants C. Bauman, B. Bergmeier, and A. Bitzel (see its history by Charles Loehr).

The Louisiana militia organizations at the outset of the Rebellion included the New Orleans Jägers, Captain Peters, Lieutenants Fassbinder and Huth; the Sharpshooters, Captain Christern; the Fusileers, Captain Sievers, Lieutenants Gerdes and Walbrack; the La Fayette Guards, Captain Koenig, Lieutenants Hollenback and Fridebach; the Jefferson Guards, Captain Wollrath, Lieutenant Lehman; Reichard's

Battalion ; Turner Guards, Captain Bahncke, Lieutenants Von Armlinsen, Eicholz, Schneider; Steuben Guards, Captain Burger, Lieutenants Kehrwald, Rosenbaum, Hausner ; Reichard Rifles, Captain Reitmeyer, Lieutenants Weise, De Petz, Muller; Louisiana Volunteers, Captain Ruhl, Lieutenants Von Zincken, Darrel ; Black Jägers, Captain Robenhorst ; Florence Guards, Captain Brummenstadt, Lieutenants Lachenmeyer, Wassernagel, Warburg. Bachman's was one of the batteries of the Washington Artillery of New Orleans, and the Tenth Louisiana was commanded by Colonel Waggaman.

In Georgia, among the troops engaged in defence of Fort Pulaski were the German Volunteers, Captain John H. Stegin, one of the companies of the First Volunteer Regiment of Georgia.

The register of the Confederate States army contains the following German names: Colonels J. T. Holtzclaw, Eighteenth Alabama, Brigadier-General ; A. H. Helvenstein, Sixteenth Alabama ; E. Waggaman, Tenth Louisiana; L. C. Gause, Thirty-second Arkansas; Major W. O. Yager, Third Texas Cavalry; Captain R. M. Gans, Fourth Texas Cavalry; Colonel J. N. Adenbousch, Second Virginia Infantry ; Colonel J. N. Waul, Tenth Texas, Brigadier-General ; Captain

F. C. Schulz, Chestnut Artillery, South Carolina; Captain C. R. Hanleiter, Jr., Thompson's Artillery, Georgia; J. A. Englehard, Major and Assistant Adjutant-General, Pender's Light Division, Third Corps; R. W. Memminger, Assistant Adjutant-General and Chief of Staff, Department of Mississippi and East Louisiana.

Gustav Schleicher was the first German in Congress, who there won reputation as a representative of the Germans of the United States. Born in Darmstadt in 1823, he studied at Giessen, became a successful civil engineer, emigrated to Texas in 1847, established himself finally in San Antonio, served, successively, in both branches of the Texas Legislature, was lieutenant-colonel and colonel of the Texas Rangers in the Confederate army, and was elected to the United States Congress in 1874 as a German Democrat. He showed marked ability, thorough training, and conscientious study. Reelected twice to Congress, his premature death in 1879 cut short a career which gave promise of honor to himself and usefulness to his adopted country.

The statistics of nativity of the population of the States at the time of the Rebellion are not to be absolutely ascertained. I find in "Freiheit u. Sklaverei unter dem Sternenbanner, oder Land u. Leute in Amerika," by Theodore Griesinger, Stuttgart, 1862, the statement that in Pennsylvania there were then over a million of German birth and descent; in New York, 800,000; in Ohio, 600,000; in New Jersey, 125,000; in New England, 30,000; while there were in the Southern States, in Virginia, 250,000; in Maryland, 125,000; in Missouri, over 100,000; in Louisiana, 50,000; in Texas, 30,000; in Tennessee, 50,000; in North Carolina and Kentucky, 70,000; in Delaware, 25,000; in South Carolina, 20,000; in the cotton States,—Georgia, Alabama, Mississippi, and Arkansas, 10,000; in Florida, 5000. There is no estimate of the number in the Northwest, that vast region from which came the volunteers of Illinois, Indiana, Michigan, Wisconsin, and Iowa. Of course the Germans of Missouri supplied large numbers of soldiers, some of them of great distinction, and many Germans from other States went to Missouri, as that was almost the first seat of active operations, and Fremont and Sigel and Asboth attracted Germans from all quarters, just as in the East, German regiments were asking to join Blenker's brigade until it became a division, and others were ready to swell the division to a corps. Indeed, it was from Blenker's demand to lead it that McClellan was obliged to administer a reproof which led finally to his resignation from active service.

The only attempt at an official analysis of the nativity of the soldiers of the Union army is that found in a volume of medical statistics published in a final report of the Provost-Marshal General, General James B. Fry, U.S.A., in which it is stated that out of 343,764 drafted men there were from Würtemberg, 1; Austria, 67; Prussia, 754; Bavaria, 35; Saxony, 15; Germany, 35,935; Switzerland, 1158; total, 37,965; but in another place it is said that there were of German birth 54,944 soldiers drafted in the service. In the same report it is said that during the Mexican war thirty per cent. of the American army were of foreign birth, and that this proportion held good of the volunteers during the Rebellion, but that in times of peace the proportions were reversed, seventy per cent. of the recruits being of foreign birth. It is also stated that twenty-four nationalities were represented in the United States army, and that out of a total of a million two hundred and fifty thousand men actually in the war, there were seventy-five thousand Germans.

This is certainly very far short of the actual number, and is by no means borne out as accurate even by the estimates made by the very competent authority of the statistician employed by the United States Sanitary Commission, Dr. B. A. Gould, whose tables are based upon very careful mathematical data, and come as near the truth as can be expected in the absence of absolute returns.

The United States Sanitary Commission, in addition to its other good work, has published "Investigations in the Statistics of American Soldiers," by B. A. Gould (New York, 1869), of which one chapter is devoted to the nativity of the United States Volunteers (chap. ii., pp. 15–26). It gives a suggestive list of the arrivals of aliens in the United States, as follows:

1860	153,640
1861	112,705
1862	114,475
1863	199,811
1864	221,535

Thirty in each hundred alien passengers before 1861, and thirty-three in each hundred during the war, were males of military age, and the total for the years of the war may be placed at two hundred and twenty-nine thousand five hundred and thirty-two.

It was not until the war had been waged for some time that the place of birth was systematically required on the enlistment rolls; the actual records are therefore very imperfect, and as many men enlisted at different times for different periods,—in one instance five times,—even regimental statistics are misleading. It was not until the organization of the provost-marshal-general's office that nativity was made an essential element of the history of each soldier. Out of the two and a half million of men in the army, the nativities of about one million two hundred thousand have been collected for Dr. Gould's work from the records at the national and State capitals, of about two hundred and ninety-three thousand from regimental officers. In Missouri it was estimated that there were ten thousand re-enlistments among the German population; but making due allowance for these, the Sanitary Commission gives the following table of Germans, volunteers in the different regiments from the States, and in the parallel column that of the proportion the Germans would have borne to the native and other nationalities in the populations of each State; and I have added the German population from the census of 1860 in another column:

From	Number of German Soldiers.	Proportion to whole Population.	Total German Population. Census of 1860.
Maine	244	34	2,601
New Hampshire	952	35	412
Vermont	86	19	219
Massachusetts	1,876	860	9,961
Rhode Island and Connecticut	2,919	824 { R. I. / Conn.	845 / 8,525
New York	36,680	22,591	256,252
New Jersey	7,387	3,097	33,772
Pennsylvania	17,208	13,173	138,244
Delaware	621	139	1,263
Maryland	3,107	2,373	43,884
District of Columbia	746	643	3,254
West Virginia	869	194 (Va.)	10,512
Kentucky	1,943	1,276	27,227
Ohio	20,102	18,984	168,210
Indiana	7,190	7,793	66,705
Illinois	18,140	16,647	130,804
Michigan	3,534	3,793	38,787
Wisconsin	15,709	12,729	123,879
Minnesota	2,715	2,172	18,400
Iowa	2,850	3,239	38,555
Missouri	30,899	7,105	88,487
Kansas	1,090	692	4,318
A grand total of	187,858	128,102	1,118,402

And as against this there were

	Proportion to Population.	Volunteers.
British Americans	22,695	53,532
English	38,250	45,508
Irish	139,052	144,221
Other foreigners	39,455	48,410
Foreigners not otherwise designated	278	26,445

Adding to these native Americans 1,523,267, makes a total of 2,018,200 soldiers whose nativity is thus established, out of the 2,500,000 in the Union army.

Part of the unwritten history of the war for the Union is the result of the firm stand the Germans took in defence of their new Fatherland. In the East, and still more in the West, before the Rebellion the German element was hardly appreciated by the mass of the people. With the outbreak of the war it asserted itself, and won a place in the consideration of their fellow-citizens that has been shown by their recognition in its government, and, to a still greater degree, in its social development. In the Southwest, notably, the Southern element was antagonistic to the Germans,—their industry, their frugality, their sobriety, their simple tastes, their love of family, their pride in their homes, were all elements of a civilization unknown in that part of the country. When the Germans answered the appeal to support and defend the Union, their uprising was a surprise. Politicians looked unkindly on their military organizations, and were indisposed to give them a place in the army. The steadiness of Blenker's division at Bull Run gave his German regiments a consideration which stood them in good stead later on, when disasters befell them at Chancellorsville and at Gettysburg. In the West, Sigel organized the German regiments and helped to save Missouri to the Union.

The Germans who had been soldiers at home, but were employed peacefully throughout the country, at the first appeal to arms hurried to join their fellow-countrymen, and many others joined them who had recently come over here to seek their fortunes, and not a few whose trade was war helped to swell the strength of the German regiments. Asboth organized a cavalry brigade, which did good service to the end. The Fourth (German) Missouri Cavalry was one of his regiments, and although its colonel and its adjutant were Americans, most of its officers and all of its rank and file were Germans, old soldiers, who soon showed their capacity to adapt the lessons of their old military experience to the new problems of the war in this country.

The scattered settlements of Germans throughout Missouri made the strength of the Union men of that State and kept it in its place. Encouraged in turn by the success of their countrymen, large numbers of new settlers followed their example, among them many who had seen the future wealth of the country even in a time of war, and that the desolating border war which carries so much misery in its course. Now throughout Western Missouri there are thriving villages and prosperous towns, connected by a network of well-tilled farms, where German is the universal element. To them the success of the Union cause was the guarantee of their future prosperity, and from their support it derived much of its best strength.

Colonel Waring's attractive little book, "Whip and Spur" (Boston, 1875), gives an admirable sketch of the life in the Fourth Missouri Cavalry. Full of grace, charming in tone and spirit, told with the true feeling of a real soldier, it shows with much more vivid truth than most professed histories the real inner life of a cavalry regiment largely made up of old German soldiers. From its lieutenant-colonel, Von Helmrich, for twenty-eight years a cavalry soldier in Germany, down to the Swiss trumpeter, all were imbued with that military spirit which makes the typical German soldier. Colonel Waring's story is one of rough campaigns, of hurrying expeditions, of hair-breadth 'scapes, of a soldier's life in a border warfare, and it will preserve the fame of the Fourth Missouri Cavalry when the dull records of many other regiments have been forgotten. It is just such a book as will serve to keep alive the best memories of the German cavalrymen in the war for the Union in the West.

The German soldier of the West and Northwest at once took his right place in the army, and won for himself and his countrymen the respect and the affection and the confidence of his native-born fellow-citizens. What was before a scanty permission has now become a matter of right, and the German, as a factor in both the political and social progress of the country, owes his place to what was done and won for it in the war of the Rebellion. Many Germans no doubt came over here as a sort of freebooters, attracted by the high pay and the rapid promotion, and all the advantages that a volunteer army enjoyed over the great standing army of their native country. Many of them settled here, when the war was over, and became good and useful citizens, ready to do their share in making their new homes prosperous and happy. Thus, whatever their sacrifices,—and they were great in life and health,—their reward has been proportionately great, and the Germans throughout the civilized world owe much of their present position, of the accepted greatness of the Empire, to the devotion, freely offered, of their services to the United States in its hour of trial, and to the example they then gave of fidelity to their political principles.

The story of the German soldier in the Rebellion is one of the characteristic features of that varying struggle. In the outset in the East the enthusiasm of the German population in their support of the Union was heartily welcome. In Missouri, under Sigel, it was their uprising that saved that State to the Union, and from the Germans of Missouri and the Northwest there came soldiers who won the day against the disloyal government of the State. Fremont rallied around him bodies of German troops of a strange sort at first, but that later on in the war became useful soldiers. In New York, Blenker raised a regiment which soon swelled to a brigade, and then to a division, and might have become an army corps. Their steadiness in protecting the retreat at the first Bull Run won for them general applause. Their camp in front of Washington, during the preparation that McClellan gave his raw troops, was a scene of military displays in the fashion of Germany, little known or appreciated by our work-a-day army, but largely admired by spectators from far and near.

The successive ill fortune of the German troops under Sigel in the valley of Virginia, and under Howard at Chancellorsville and Gettysburg, was fully atoned for by their share in the operations under Sherman. From being overpraised at the outset they were afterwards unjustly overblamed, and the truth undoubtedly rested between the two extremes. There were incompetent officers and inefficient soldiers in their number in the outset, but these were gradually weeded out, and in the end it can fairly be said that the German soldiers in the Rebellion contributed largely to the success that finally crowned the war. To give a detailed account of so large a number, scattered over such an extent of country, would be impossible, but a few shining examples may serve the purpose.

In a pamphlet issued by the War Department in 1885, there is given the local designation of volunteer organizations in the United States army during the war of the Rebellion, 1860–65, which is of interest, as showing in part the nationality of troops.

In New York:

Dickel's Mounted Rifles, Fourth New York Cavalry.

Blenker's Battery, Second Battery Light Artillery, New York.

Steuben Regiment, Seventh New York Infantry.

First German Rifles, Eighth New York Infantry.

United Turner Rifles, Twentieth New York Infantry.

First Astor Regiment, Twenty-ninth New York Infantry.

Fifth German Rifles, Forty-fifth New York Infantry.

Fremont Regiment, Forty-sixth New York Infantry.

Sigel Rifles, or German Rangers, Fifty-second New York Infantry.

Barney Rifles, or Schwartze Yäger Regiment, Fifty-fourth New York Infantry.

Steuben Rangers, Eighty-sixth New York Infantry.

In Pennsylvania:

First German Regiment, Seventy-fourth Pennsylvania Infantry.

Second German Regiment, Seventy-fifth Pennsylvania Infantry.

In Ohio:

First German Regiment, Twenty-eighth Ohio Infantry.

Second German Regiment, Thirty-seventh Ohio Infantry, Colonel Siber.

Third German Regiment, Sixty-seventh Ohio Infantry, Colonel Burstenbinder.

In Indiana:

First German Regiment, Thirty-second Indiana, commanded, successively, by Willich, Von Trebra, and Erdelmeyer.

In Illinois:

Hecker's Yäger Regiment, Twenty-fourth Illinois.

In Wisconsin:

First German Regiment, Ninth Wisconsin.

Second German Regiment, Twenty-sixth Wisconsin.

Bates's History of the Pennsylvania Regiments, etc., in the Rebellion, is a huge work of five enormous volumes, and from its endless pages there is much material to be gathered bearing on the German element in the war. Pennsylvania naturally claims for its citizens of German descent, including those whose ancestors were among the early settlers, a place in any tribute to the German soldiers. Among the first five companies organized in Pennsylvania at the very outset, there were many Pennsylvania Germans; and of the twenty-five regiments raised for the three months' service, there were the Fourth, with Hartranft as its colonel, from Norristown and Pottstown; the Eighth, from Lehigh and Northampton; the Ninth, from Chester and Delaware, with Pennypacker; the Tenth, from Lancaster; the Eleventh, from Northumberland; the Fourteenth, from Berks; the Fifteenth, from Luzerne; the Sixteenth, from York and Schuylkill; the Eighteenth, in Philadelphia, under Wilhelm; the Twenty-first, under Ballier, largely made up of Germans.

Of the three-year regiments, those who bore the brunt of the war, there was the Twenty-seventh, which gained credit from and for Bushbeck; while of the fifteen regiments of the Pennsylvania Reserves, the largest organized force, indeed the only division sent by one State to the field, many of its members were Germans by birth or descent,—and so, too, of the Forty-eighth, from Schuylkill; the Fiftieth, from Berks; the Fifty-first, under Hartranft, from Montgomery; the Fifty-sixth, under Hoffman; the Sixty-fifth, better known as the Fifth Cavalry; the Seventy-fourth, from Pittsburg; the Seventy-fifth, under Bohlen; the Seventy-ninth, from Lancaster; the Eighty-eighth, from Berks and Philadelphia, with General Louis Wagner; the Ninety-sixth, from Schuylkill; the Ninety-seventh, under Pennypacker, from Chester and Delaware; the Ninety-eighth, the old Twenty-first reorganized, under Ballier, thoroughly German in rank and file; the One Hundred and Twelfth, or Second Artillery,—so large a regiment that out of it a second regiment was organized; the One Hundred and Thirteenth, or Twelfth Cavalry, and the One Hundred and Fifty-second, or Third Artillery,— almost distinctively German. Then there were the One Hundred and Thirtieth, from York; the One Hundred and Thirty-first, from Northumberland; and the One Hundred and Fifty-third, from Northampton,—it was brigaded under Sigel, Stahel, and Von Gilsa, with the New York regiments of Salm,

Holmstedt, and Von Amsberg, and the Eighty-second Illinois, of Hecker,—nothing could point more conclusively to the German element in the war than such names as these.

The One Hundred and Sixty-eighth Pennsylvania Volunteers, from Berks, was organized and commanded by Charles A. Knoderer.

This is a fair proportion of the two hundred and fifteen regiments, nine batteries, two independent companies, and eleven colored regiments raised in Pennsylvania, and even a hasty glance at the long list of names of officers and men of the successive regiments will show a large German element scattered throughout them. One of the best elements of the little regular army was the supply of excellent non-commissioned officers, largely old German soldiers, and it was a great stroke of good fortune when a volunteer company had one of these well-trained and well-disciplined men in its ranks,—he steadied the whole line, and gave it an example of soldierly excellence in every particular.

Such a man was Edward Scherer, first sergeant of Company B, of the One Hundred and Twenty-first Pennsylvania Volunteers,—a German who had served in a battery of the Third United States Artillery, under some of the most distinguished officers of the regular army. Such men as Reynolds and Burnside recognized him as an old comrade, and his bearing and gallantry and knowledge of the real business of soldiering were the object of universal admiration among the green hands, both officers and men, of his regiment. He fell at the battle of Fredericksburg, Virginia, and he was but a type of that large number of German soldiers who served in the ranks, and who, like Scherer, sacrificed good employment at home to do their duty to the country of their adoption at its hour of supreme peril and trial.

A characteristic and distinguished example of the services rendered by our Pennsylvanians of German descent is the brilliant career of General G. Pennypacker, of the Ninth and the Ninety-seventh Pennsylvania Volunteers. Born in 1842, at Valley Forge, he was one of the descendants of Heinrich Pannebäcker, who came to America from Germany before 1699, and settled on Skippack Creek. Many of this family settled in the adjoining counties of Montgomery, Chester, and Berks, and of the later generations not a few found their way into Virginia, Kentucky, Tennessee, and Mississippi, where their names are found in positions of importance and trust.

On the rolls of those who served in the Revolution and the later wars of the Republic, there are many representatives of this old German stock. The Pennypacker war record is a notable one. During the Revolution this family had as its representatives in the Continental army, a captain, an ensign, a lieutenant, a corporal, and a private. In the war of 1812 it had two of its members in the field; in the Mexican war, three. In the war of the Rebellion it furnished to the Union army two major-generals, one adjutant-general, one colonel, one surgeon, one assistant surgeon, two captains, one lieutenant, five sergeants, eight corporals, one musician, and sixty-five privates. To the Southern army it gave one lieutenant-colonel, one quartermaster, four captains, five lieutenants, and twenty-eight enlisted men,—a total of one hundred and twenty-eight. No doubt this list could be increased if all branches of the old stock reported their military contingent. At all events it is worth pointing out, that others may try to parallel it by a diligent search through their own records for other examples of the kind. The great-grandfather of General Pennypacker was a bishop of the Mennonite Church ; his father was on the staff of General Worth in the Mexican war. At the age of eighteen, after he had begun life as a printer, young Pennypacker became a member of a local volunteer company, and marched with it to Harrisburg on the first summons for troops in 1861, serving with it in the Ninth Regiment. He soon became captain and then major of the reorganized regiment in the three-years' service, the Ninety-seventh, and bravely fought his way through the war, became colonel of the regiment, was soon put in command of a brigade, won his star as a brigadier-general for his gallantry at the capture of Fort Fisher, at twenty-two was the youngest general officer in the war, and was brevetted a major-general. In 1866 he quietly settled down to study law, when he was appointed colonel of the Thirty-fourth Infantry in the regular army, then assigned to the Sixteenth; he was the youngest colonel in the regular army, and finally retired in 1883 at an age when with most men a career of distinction such as his is usually just beginning.

Zinn, of the One Hundred and Thirtieth; Schall, of the Fifty-first, one of eight brothers in the army; Brenholz, of the Fiftieth; Gries, of the One Hundred and Fourth; Kohler, of the Ninety-eighth, were all of Pennsylvania birth, but of German descent. Knoderer, of the One Hundred and Sixty-eighth, was born in Baden, was educated at Carlsruhe, at the Polytechnical School, and left the service of the government to join Sigel's force in the unsuccessful revolution of 1849. In Reading (Pennsylvania) he found a new home and employment as a civil engineer; but when the Rebellion broke out he went first as a captain of engineers on Sigel's staff, then enlisted as a private and was elected colonel of the Eleventh Pennsylvania, and afterwards was appointed colonel of the One Hundred and Sixty-eighth Pennsylvania, and fell at its head on the 30th January, 1863, near Suffolk, Virginia.

Ballier was born in Würtemberg in 1815; studied at the Military School at Stuttgard in 1833–34; settled in Philadelphia, where he was a member of the Washington Guard, the first German military organization in the North, in 1836; enlisted as a private in the First Pennsylvania for the Mexican war, was made major for his services there,—then was colonel of the Twenty-first and of the Ninety-eighth for the Rebellion. Twice seriously wounded, he still remains with us to renew the recollection of his varied experiences, a veteran of many battles.

Hartranft's commission as brigadier-general was won by his services at Bull Run, Antietam, Fredericksburg; and as the hero of Fort Stedman he became a major-general. His services in civil life have been equally distinguished, and his career is marked by well-earned honors, as Governor of Pennsylvania, as the chief representative of the Federal Government in Philadelphia, and as the head of the State militia.

Everard Bierer, colonel of the One Hundred and Seventy-first Pennsylvania, was the son of German parents, settled in Fayette County. He won his first successes in the Eleventh Pennsylvania Reserves, was appointed by Governor Curtin to be colonel of the One Hundred and Seventy-first, and was promoted to the command of a brigade. Now he is a successful lawyer, legislator, and farmer in Kansas.

Colonel Lehmann, of the One Hundred and Third, was born in Hanover in 1812, was educated there at the military school, served for six years in the army, and in 1837 came to Pittsburg, where he became a teacher. He organized the Sixty-second Pennsylvania, was its lieutenant-colonel, then was colonel of the One Hundred and Third, and after the war resumed his work of education, and became president of the Western Pennsylvania Military Academy.

The Wistars who served in the war by the half a score were all of that good old German stock whose representatives are so well and honorably known in every walk of life in their native city and far beyond it.

Philadelphia sent General Isaac J. Wistar, colonel of the Seventy-first Pennsylvania; Major Joseph W. Wistar, of the Eighth Pennsylvania Cavalry; Colonel Francis Wistar, captain of the Twelfth United States Infantry, and colonel of the Two Hundred and Fifteenth Pennsylvania; Colonel Langhorne Wistar, captain of the First Pennsylvania Rifles, "Bucktails," colonel of the One Hundred and Fiftieth Pennsylvania, and brevet brigadier-general; Colonel William Rotch Wistar, of the Twentieth Pennsylvania Cavalry.

William Doster, colonel of the Fourth Cavalry, was born in Bethlehem, Pennsylvania, where his father, a native of Swabia, settled in 1817, marrying the daughter of a Vorsteher of the Brethren's House, the granddaughter of a Revolutionary soldier. A graduate of Yale of '57, and of the Harvard Law School of '59, he studied law in Heidelberg and Paris. Returning to this country, he became major of the Fourth Pennsylvania Cavalry, led it in the Chancellorsville and Gettysburg campaigns, and was promoted for his services.

General J. William Hofmann, colonel of the Fifty-sixth Pennsylvania, was the son of Prussian parents, who settled in Philadelphia in 1819. Long an active member of local militia organizations, he went to the field a thorough soldier, and his career was one of distinguished gallantry, characterized alike by merit and modesty. The opinion of all his superior officers was an unbroken and unanimous approval of his ability and his courage, and he deserves, as he has won, and he enjoys, the respect of his fellow-citizens for the distinguished services he rendered in all the responsible positions assigned him during his long period of active service.

General Adolph Bushbeck was born in Coblenz, Prussia, in 1822, the son of a German officer. From his eleventh to his seventeenth year he was at the cadet school in Berlin, then became ensign and lieutenant, and at the suggestion of Steinwehr was appointed instructor at the cadet school at Potsdam, from 1847 to 1852. In 1853 he came to Philadelphia, and was well and favorably known as a successful teacher. When the Rebellion broke out he became major, and later colonel of the Twenty-seventh Pennsylvania, and in that and his successive commands, as general of brigade and division, won unstinted praise for his high soldierly qualities. From General Sherman he received warm commendation. The war over, he returned to Philadelphia, and resumed his former occupation for some years, and then, going abroad with his family, died in Florence, Italy, in 1883.

Henry Bohlen was born in Bremen in 1810. As early as 1831, on the recommendation of Lafayette, he was appointed on the staff of General Gerard, and served during the siege of Antwerp. In the Mexican war he served on the staff of General Worth, and took part in many engagements. In the Crimean war he served in the French army, and at the outbreak of the Rebellion, returning from Europe, where he was living in great splendor, enjoying a large fortune and a brilliant social position, he raised the Seventy-fifth, a German regiment, mainly at his own expense, and led it with such distinguished gallantry that he was commended in warm terms by Fremont and Sigel, under whom he served, and was soon appointed a brigadier-general. His brilliant career ended in his death in action, in August, 1862.

The Vezins—Oscar, Henry, Alfred—served with credit in various branches of the service, always doing honor to a name that belongs to one of the oldest merchants of Philadelphia in its days of greatness as a commercial city.

Henry Vezin was captain Company G, Fifth Pennsylvania Cavalry; Alfred, captain Company C, Fifteenth Pennsylvania Cavalry, and afterwards adjutant Fourth Missouri Cavalry.

The name of General John A. Koltes is perpetuated in that of the Post No. 228 of the Grand Army of the Republic, which thus does due honor to that gallant soldier. He organized the Seventy-third Regiment, originally known as the Pennsylvania Legion, Forty-fifth of the line. It was recruited in Philadelphia, in June and July, 1861, and was first at a rendezvous at Lemon Hill. Colonel Koltes, Lieutenant-Colonel Muehleck, Major Schott, were the field-officers. It joined Blenker's division in September, and went with it through the West Virginia campaign under Fremont and Sigel, and then under Pope into the second Bull Run. Koltes was in command of the brigade, and Brueckner of the regiment, when they both fell in action on the 30th of August, 1862, gallantly leading their men against an overwhelming force. General Schurz, in his report as division commander, commends the conduct of Koltes and his brigade, temporarily attached to his division. It consisted of the Sixty-eighth New York, the Twenty-ninth New York, and the Seventy-third Pennsylvania, with Dilger's Battery. He says, "The gallant Koltes died a noble death at the head of his brave regiments," and he deplores "the brave and noble Koltes." General Sigel, who commanded the First Corps, regrets, in his report, "the death of the intrepid Koltes."

General Koltes was born in Treves in 1827, and came to this country while he was still a lad, in his seventeenth year. He became a teacher in a Catholic institute in Pittsburg, enlisted in 1846 as a volunteer in the Mexican war, and afterwards in the regular army. On his return he was employed in the United States Mint, became a member of the Scott Legion, and took an active part in the local militia. He drilled the Männerchor Rifle Guards for home service, and recruited a regiment for the war. He received a commission as brigadier-general, and it was at the head of his brigade that he fell in action at the second Bull Run. Koltes was, like Ballier, Binder, and Bohlen, one of the active spirits in the early military organizations in Philadelphia. Besides the Philadelphia regiments, they furnished for the war four companies of Philadelphia Turners, who joined their comrades in the Turner Regiment, organized in New York under Colonel Soest, and many went into New Jersey regiments and those of other States.

Among the young Germans of Philadelphia, Fritz Tiedeman has a high place for his gallant services. He was, successively, quartermaster-sergeant, second lieutenant, adjutant, and captain of the Seventy-fifth Pennsylvania, and then on the staff of General Schurz; and his brother, who fell early in the war, gave promise of equal merit.

General Louis Wagner was born in Giessen, Germany, in 1838, and came to Philadelphia as a lad with his father, a revolutionary refugee, in 1849. Educated at the public schools, in 1861 he entered the service as a first lieutenant of the Eighty-eighth Pennsylvania Volunteers, and at the close was colonel of the regiment and a brevet brigadier-general. Returning to civil life, he organized the Grand Army of the Republic in Pennsylvania, in 1879, and has been one of the leading men of that organization ever since. He has taken a very active part in other civil and military bodies, and has been honored by many elective offices and appointments, all of which he has filled with characteristic zeal and energy.

New York, as the gathering place of all nationalities, naturally sent many Germans to the army. The Thirty-ninth, or Garibaldi Guard, consisted of three companies of Germans, three of Hungarians, one each of Swiss, Italians, and French, and one of Spanish and Portuguese.

The Seventh Regiment Infantry, New York State Volunteers, or "Steuben Rangers," organized by Colonel John E. Bendix, and reorganized by Colonel G. von Schach, had, as its original officers, Lieutenant-Colonel Edward Kapff, Major C. Keller, and Captains Goebel, Boecht, Brestel, Pfeiffer, Anselm, Hocheimer, S. L. Kapff, Schonleber, Bethan, Wratislau.

The Eighth, or "First German Rifles," was organized by Blenker, who commanded a brigade at the first Bull Run, and a division under Fremont in the valley campaign. It was in Sigel's corps in the second Battle of Bull Run.

The Twentieth, or "United Turner Rifles," was organized by the New York Turn-Verein, in April, 1861, from its societies. German citizens provided the money for its expenses; a committee of ladies, called the "Turner-sisters," supplied many necessaries. Max Weber was its colonel, Franz Weiss lieutenant-colonel, and Englebert Schnepf major.

The Twenty-ninth, or "Astor Rifles," was organized by Steinwehr, who, in his farewell order, says it was the last to leave the field at Bull Run, and served with distinction under Fremont, Sigel, and at Chancellorsville, and earned a place in the history of the war.

The Fifth New York State Militia was a German organization,—its officers were, Colonel Schwarzwalder, Lieutenant-Colonel Burger, Major von Amsberg.

Of the Forty-first, or De Kalb Guards, Colonel von Gilsa, seven hundred of its men had been in the Prussian service in the Schleswig-Holstein war. One company was raised in Philadelphia, and another in Newark, New Jersey.

The Fifty-second Regiment Infantry, New York State Volunteers, was organized at Staten Island, New York, in the autumn of 1861, by the consolidation of four companies of the "Sigel Rifles," and six companies of the "German Rangers," under Colonel Paul Frank.

The commanders of companies were:

A. Captain Charles G. Freudenberg.

B. Captain Henry L. Klein.
C. Captain Gustave Schultze.
D. Captain Oscar von Schoening.
E. Captain J. C. Messerschmidt.
F. Captain Charles Mohring.
G. Captain O. C. Garwin.
H. Captain Jacob Rueger.
I. Captain Adolphus Becker.
K. Captain Francis Benzler.

The lieutenant-colonel was Louis Kasouzki; major, Philip C. Lichtenstein.

A national flag, a regimental flag, and two guidons were presented by the German ladies of New York.

It formed part of the Third Brigade, First Division, Second Corps, was brigaded with the Fifty-seventh and Sixty-sixth New York, and Fifty-third Pennsylvania, under Sumner, French, Zook, and Frank.

At Antietam it lost its lieutenant-colonel, Lichtenstein; at Gettysburg, its brigade commander, Zook; in the Wilderness campaign under Hancock, two gallant Germans, Count Hacke and Baron von Steuben, both officers of the Prussian army, serving as volunteers in that of the Union. Count Hacke was a brave and gentle comrade, of kind, modest, and unassuming manners, endeared to his fellow-soldiers by his manly virtues. His epitaph is written in the hearts of all who knew him, as a brave and true soldier, who fell in battle for a noble cause.

In October of 1864, the remnant of the original Fifty-second, five officers and thirty-five men, under Major Retzius, returned to New York. Colonel Frank, promoted to be a brigadier-general, was succeeded by Colonel Karples, and under him the regiment was finally mustered out in July, 1865. Of the two thousand eight hundred whose names appear on its rolls, only two hundred returned; thirty-four of its officers were killed or disabled during its four years of service.

The Military Order of the Loyal Legion is for the Union army what the Society of the Cincinnati was for the Revolutionary army. Its records preserve and perpetuate the memories of many gallant soldiers. Among them is to be found a sketch of the life and services of Carl Gottfried Freudenberg. Born in Heidelberg, Germany, May 1, 1833, at an early age he entered the military service as a cadet in the Carlsruhe School. While there the revolution of 1848 broke out, and, although but fifteen, he took the field with his fellow-students, and was engaged in the battle fought near Mannheim. As his mind matured it developed such conclusions upon political liberty as impelled him to forego brilliant prospects of preferment, and he came to the United States a few years before the great Rebellion. When a call was issued for soldiers he raised a company of infantry, and with it entered the service as captain of the Fifty-second New York Volunteer Infantry, August 3, 1861. On the 9th of November he became its major, and was severely wounded at the battle of Fair Oaks. On November 24, 1862, he was promoted lieutenant-colonel, and commanded his regiment at Chancellorsville and Gettysburg, where he was again desperately wounded. Forced to leave the field by his injuries, he resigned his commission in the Fifty-second New York and accepted an appointment as major in the Veteran Reserve Corps, organized the Twenty-third Regiment, and on April 22, 1864, became its lieutenant-colonel, serving in the Bureau of Refugees, Freedmen, and Abandoned Lands, as commandant at Milwaukee, as inspector-general and commandant of the District of Wisconsin. On the reorganization of the army he was appointed captain of the Forty-fifth (Veteran Reserve) Infantry; in 1869 was transferred to the Fourteenth

Infantry, was brevetted colonel of volunteers, and as major and lieutenant-colonel of the regular army. In May, 1870, he went with his regiment to the Northwest, to quell a threatened Indian outbreak, but in December he was obliged to go on the retired list as captain, and in 1877 he was promoted lieutenant-colonel. He died in Washington, August 28, 1885, enjoying the confidence and affection of all who knew him, as the very embodiment of personal honor and soldierly virtue.

One of the most effective services rendered the cause of the Union was the long series of political cartoons furnished to *Harper's Weekly* during the civil war by Thomas Nast, born on the Rhine in 1840. His pencil was recognized far and wide as that of a sturdy champion, and his productions were heartily welcomed by the soldiers in the field and by earnest patriots everywhere. Thomas Nast was born in Landau, Bavaria, September 27, 1840, and came with his mother to New York in 1846, and was there joined in 1849 by his father, who had served on the man-of-war "Ohio." He began to work on Frank Leslie's illustrated paper, studied in the Academy of Design, made a campaign with Garibaldi in 1860, sending sketches to the New York,

London, and Paris illustrated papers, returning to New York in 1861. His contributions to *Harper's Weekly* became historical, and have received the well-merited praise of historians and art critics. They were useful in keeping alive the loyal feeling of the North, and received the hearty plaudits of the soldiers in the field. When peace was restored he won new honors in the civil contest that waged over Andrew Johnson's administration, and even now he fights for good government with his pencil.

The Princess Salm-Salm, in her book, "Ten Years of My Life,"—and a very adventurous one it was,—describes the camp of the German division (Blenker's) in front of Washington, in the fall of 1861, as the principal point of attraction. It consisted of about twelve thousand men, under Blenker and Steinwehr, who had gained great credit for protecting the retreat from the first Bull Run. Blenker was born in Tours, had served in the Bavarian army and in that of Greece under its Bavarian king, took part in the German revolution of '48, fled to Switzerland, then came to New York, and was farming when the Rebellion broke out. He raised the Eighth New York, and Prussian and Austrian soldiers furnished a considerable proportion of its officers, among them

Prince Salm-Salm, who served to the end of the war, then in Mexico, and finally fell in the Franco-Prussian war. Another of his officers was Corvin, who, after six years in Prussian prisons as a penalty for his share in the German revolution, came to this country as the war correspondent of the London *Times* and the Augsburger *Allgemeine Zeitung.*

Among other German officers were von der Groeben; von Schack, colonel of the Seventh New York; von Buggenhagen, one of its captains; von Radowitz, Schwenke, Gerber, Max Weber; Schirmer, chief of artillery of the Eleventh Corps; von Puttkammer, of the Third Corps; von Amsberg, von Gilsa, von Kusserow, von Kleisser; von Schrader, of the Seventy-fourth Ohio, killed in action; von Trebra, of the Thirty-second Indiana; and Leppien, lieutenant-colonel of the First Maine Artillery, one of the most gallant soldiers, from Philadelphia.

Carl Schurz was the first colonel of the first regiment of volunteer cavalry duly authorized to be raised. On his way to New York he found Chorman's Rangers also inviting recruits, while other cavalry companies were being busily raised in Philadelphia. In New York he found additional countrymen at work,—Frederick von Schickfuss, August

Haurand, Count Haake, von Blankenburg, Bern de Tavergnier, von Strautz, von Veltheim, Count Ferdinand Storch, and Count von Moltke, Hendricks, Passegger, Hertzog,—who soon found plenty of men. Schurz himself went to Spain as minister, and the regiment was fortunate in having for its first colonel in the field A. T. M. Reynolds, a very good, experienced soldier. The four companies of Germans were all old soldiers. Their record through the war is a very creditable one, and the First New York Cavalry did its work so well that Germans may be proud of their countrymen in it both from New York and Pennsylvania.

The German element in the cavalry and artillery went far to make both of these arms of the service efficient and capable. In every regiment of cavalry and in every battery of artillery there were found old German soldiers, trained in a way that made them models for the green recruits, and instructors alike of officers and men. In most of the regiments of the regular army there were privates and non-commissioned officers, Germans by birth and soldiers by training, who were looked on with the respect that courage and discipline always secure. Many of them were promoted to commissions, and some of them commanded volunteer regiments with great credit. One of the most notable trained and veteran German soldiers was Adolph von Steinwehr, who was born September 25, 1825, at Blankenburg in Brunswick. His father was a major, his grandfather a lieutenant-general. He studied in the military school, became a lieutenant, came to the United States, and served as an officer of an Alabama regiment during the Mexican war. He was employed as an engineer by the United States, married in Mobile, returned to Germany, and then became a farmer in Connecticut. At the outbreak of the civil war he became colonel of the Twenty-ninth New York, part of the Germans that excited interest and admiration by their steadiness at the first Bull Run. This led to the organization of a German division under Blenker,—the First Brigade under Stahel: the Eighth, Wutschel; Thirty-ninth, D'Utassy; and Forty-fifth, von Amsberg, New York; and Twenty-seventh Pennsylvania, Bushbeck; Second Brigade, Steinwehr: Twenty-ninth, Kozlay; Fifty-fourth, Kryzanowsky; Fifty-eighth, Gellman, New York; Seventy-third Pennsylvania, Koltes; Third Brigade, Bohlen: Forty-first, Von Gilsa, and Sixty-eighth New York, Klecfisch; Seventy-fourth, Schimmelpfennig; Seventy-fifth

Pennsylvania, Mahler; Fourth New York Cavalry, Dickel; batteries of Schirmer, Wilderich, and Sturmfels. There were changes in the organization in which Sigel and Schurz obtained successive commands. Finally at Chancellorsville the tide turned, and the Germans of the Eleventh Corps were spoken of as if the ill-fortune of the battle was due to them. Steinwehr, however, was always honored for the conduct of his troops, and at Gettysburg again his military reputation was enhanced by his services. Under Sherman he won fresh honors in the West, and served in the army until the close of the war. From that time until his death in 1877 he was engaged in the work of authorship on subjects for which his thorough training especially fitted him. His character was marked by many manly qualities, and his name is an enduring example of German patriotism, soldiership, and culture.

Leopold von Gilsa, colonel of the Forty-first New York Volunteers, the De Kalb regiment, was a typical German soldier. Born in Prussia in 1825, the son of a Prussian officer, he served in that army, for which he was specially educated, became a major in the Schleswig-Holstein war, and soon afterwards came to this country. He was peaceably employed in teaching when the Rebellion broke out, and then he organized his regiment, and won for it the distinction of a thoroughly well-disciplined and capable body of good soldiers. Wounded at Cross Keys, he gained the confidence and admiration of his superiors by the way in which he handled his regiment and the brigade, and by his services as chief of staff to General Sigel when he was in command of the Eleventh and Twelfth Corps. He served until 1864, when he was mustered out as colonel, although he had served as commander of brigade and division. Returning to civil life, he died in New York in 1870, in consequence of the wounds and exposure incidental to four years of almost uninterrupted campaign life, marches, and battles. Gilsa Post, No. 264, of the Grand Army of the Republic, fitly marks by the adoption of his name the honor intended to be paid his memory by those who could best appreciate his services to his adopted country and his example of the devotion of his life to the cause in which he and his countrymen were united.

The First New York Battalion of Light Artillery, known as Brickel's Artillery, was composed of four batteries, all Germans,—Major Brickel, Captains Dietrich, Voegelin, Knierim, and Kusserow. After Antietam, where Major Arndt, commander of the battalion, was killed, the batteries were made independent, and were numbered Twenty-ninth, Thirtieth, Thirty-first, and Thirty-second. The Twenty-ninth was afterwards consolidated with the Thirty-second, Captain von Kusserow. Captain Kleisser was promoted to command of the Thirtieth, and the Thirty-first was subsequently consolidated with the Thirtieth. In 1865, Kusserow was appointed colonel of the Second Regiment of Hancock's Veteran Corps. The Twenty-ninth and Thirty-second Batteries were consolidated with the Fourth and Fifteenth Independent Batteries, but retained the number Thirty-second. Von Kusserow was an old officer of the Prussian army, the son of General von Kusserow. He died in Philadelphia, and was buried in presence of the German consul, Major Mergenthaler, and H. Dieck, his old comrades in arms.

Colorado had forty-two Germans in the Second Regiment, besides others whose nationalities are given as Austria, Prussia, Poland, Denmark, Sweden, Russia, Norway, Bohemia, Saxony, Holland, Bavaria, and Switzerland; so that even on the borders the proportion of foreigners was a very large one.

Among the notable officers from Illinois, besides

Hecker, whose memory deserves especial mention, there was General Knobelsdorff, a graduate of the military school at Culm, Prussia, who was a lieutenant in the Prussian army, joined the Schleswig-Holstein army, and came with hundreds of his comrades to the United States in 1851. He lived in Milwaukee and Chicago, and when the Rebellion broke out organized the Twenty-fourth and Forty-fourth Illinois, commanded a brigade in Sigel's corps, under Asboth, and had under him Colonel Nicholas Greusel, of the Seventh and Thirty-sixth Illinois, and Colonel Julius C. Raith, of the Forty-third. The Thirteenth Illinois Cavalry was also largely a German organization.

Adolph Engelmann served in the Mexican war in the Second Illinois, and during the Rebellion was colonel of the Forty-third Illinois, receiving the appointment of brigadier-general as a reward.

His predecessor in the Forty-third Illinois, Julius Raith, was born in Germany in 1820, came to the United States in 1837, served as lieutenant in the Second Illinois in the Mexican war, was promoted to captain, and, good Democrat as he had been, was ready to serve in the war for the Union as colonel of the Forty-third,—a German regiment largely organized by Gustav Körner. He fell at Shiloh, in command of a brigade.

Hugo Wangelin was educated at the military school of Berlin, came to the United States in 1834, served in the Twelfth Missouri, under Osterhaus, and succeeded him in command of the regiment when Osterhaus was promoted, making a reputation for distinguished gallantry for himself and his German soldiers, representatives of the best elements of German emigration in the West. Wangelin took part in twenty-eight engagements, and died in 1883.

Gustav Körner was a leading spirit in all German organizations in the West, both in peace and war, and his term of office as governor was marked by many events of importance.

Körner himself is a representative German, and his earnest efforts to advance German culture and to engraft it on American patriotism deserve hearty recognition. His services in organizing troops and in the executive chair of Illinois are well known. His name is honorably perpetuated in his book describing the successive and successful settlement of Germans throughout the United States. He has represented his adopted country creditably abroad, and is now among the veterans around whom cluster the association of all that is best, alike in German and American patriotism.

Thielemann's cavalry battalion and Hotaling's company of the Second Illinois Cavalry, and Stolleman's and D'Osband's and Gumbart's artillery, are among the German organizations that received frequent and always honorable mention in the history of the Western campaigns.

Gumbart's Battery, Second Illinois Light Artillery, was organized by Captain Adolph Schwarz, a son of Major-General Schwarz, of Baden. He was severely wounded at Shiloh. The first lieutenant was M. W. Mann, now a citizen of Texas.

Friedrich Hecker is one of the names that unite Germany and America in a common love of liberty. Born in Baden in 1811, educated at Heidelberg and Munich, he became a leader of the Republican party in his native country, and was recognized as one of the master-spirits of the outbreak of 1848. To its failure we owe the large accession of many Germans, whose part in the Union cause has become one of the brightest pages of our history. His welcome to his new fatherland was hearty and universal. He settled down to a quiet farmer's life in Illinois, took an active share in the work of the Republican party, enlisted at the outbreak of the Rebellion in Sigel's regiment in St. Louis, and commanded, successively, the Twenty-fourth and the Eighty-second Illinois Volunteers, and left the field only because he was so severely wounded that he could no longer serve in the army. Like Carl Schurz, he was invited to return to Germany to take part in the organization of its unity as an empire, but his love of America and American freedom made it impossible for him to leave his home. He was a representative man among the Germans, active in all their best work in civil life, and his death, on the 22d of September, 1881, called forth universal expression of grief and sorrow. At his grave, and afterwards at the dedication of a monument to his memory in St. Louis, his old associates and his younger admirers bore testimony to the respect and affection in which Hecker's name was held. Sigel, Schurz, Körner, Thielemann, Rombauer, Stifel, Ledergerber, Englemann, and many who had fought together on both continents for Republican principles, attested the service done to constitutional liberty in Europe and America by Friedrich Hecker, and the gratitude of Germany and of all Germans alike in the old and the new fatherland.

Colonel Emile Frey, the Swiss minister to the United States, was an officer of Hecker's Illinois regiments, the Twenty-fourth and Eighty-second,—he volunteered, and was a lieutenant in the former and became a major in the latter, thus serving as a soldier in two republics, that of his native Switzerland and in that of his temporary home. The son of a distinguished Liberal leader in the Canton of Basel, the father was fortunate enough in his old age to see him a soldier in the American Republic, and later the diplomatic representative of that of Switzerland in Washington. Colonel Frey's return to the United States was made the occasion of a hearty welcome alike from his countrymen and from his fellow-soldiers, and his well-earned reputation as a soldier in defence of the American Union was heightened by his able management of the interests of the Swiss Confederation in the United States. The tie that unites the two republics was greatly strengthened by this marked instance of the good service rendered the Union cause by its Swiss soldiers. A sketch of a Swiss company of sharpshooters serving during the war was printed at Richtersweil, Switzerland, in 1865, under the title, "Drei Jahre in der Potomac-armee oder eine Schweitzer Schützen Compagnie im Nordamerikanischen Kriege" (8vo, pp. 228). The report made to the Swiss Confederation by its veteran General Dufour is one of the best accounts of the Federal forces at the outset, and the visit of that gallant soldier is still remembered by all who met him during his stay in this country.

Iowa has preserved in the reports of the adjutant-general of the State a list of the places of nativity of its soldiers. Germany, of course, has its representatives in almost every organization, and in the Sixteenth and Twenty-sixth Iowa Volunteers there were companies entirely composed of Germans, rank and file, while the Fifth Cavalry was composed in part of Germans enlisted at Dubuque and Burlington for the Fremont Guards, by Colonel Carl Schaefer de Boernstein, who fell in action in Tennessee in May, 1862, and was mourned as a gallant soldier.

Matthes's Iowa battalion won distinction in Sherman's army. Colonel Nicholas Perczel, of the Tenth Iowa, was also commended as an excellent soldier.

From the French colonists settled at Icaria, in Iowa, came a number of soldiers, among them Anton von Gaudain, who was born in Berlin, of French-Huguenot stock,—the son of an army officer, and himself trained for an army officer. He came to the

United States at twenty-five, edited a French paper in New York, taught school, joined the Icarian community in Icaria, served for three years in the Union army, and after the war made his home in Corning, Iowa, near a settlement of French Icarians, where he died, in 1883. He was a scholar of remarkable attainments, and was beloved by all who knew him.

Connecticut had in its Sixth Regiment a company of Germans from New Haven, Norwich, and Waterbury, commanded by Captain Klein, who became lieutenant-colonel of the regiment, and another, under Captain Biebel, from Bridgeport, Meriden, and New York. In its Eleventh Regiment, Captain Moegling had a company of Germans from New Haven and Fairfield.

Indiana, according to the report of the adjutant-general of that State, had in its volunteer regiments 6456 Germans,—not far short of the 7190 credited to the State by Dr. Gould after the war had enabled him to make a fuller comparison of figures,—and a fair proportion of the 14,940 foreigners serving in and for that State, and of the 155,578 of its volunteer soldiers. Among the most noteworthy of its representative German soldiers were General August Willich, and Colonel John Gerber, killed in command of the Twenty-fourth Indiana at Shiloh, April 7, 1862.

A German, Albert Lange, was one of the active staff of Governor Morton, and worked faithfully to enable that State to do its share successfully in the war of the Rebellion. Another German, John B. Lutz, led the Indiana forces in their resistance to Morgan's raids. The Thirty-second was a distinctive German regiment, organized in Dearborn, Floyd, Fort Wayne, Jefferson, and other farming districts, from the best classes of German-American settlers.

Kentucky had many Germans among its fifty-six thousand loyal soldiers, and just as the Germans saved St. Louis and Missouri to the Union, so they helped to keep Louisville and Kentucky out of the Confederacy. F. Bierbower was major of the Fortieth Kentucky. Von Kielmansegge served in cavalry commands in Missouri, Florida, and Maryland, where von Koerber was also a major of the First Cavalry.

Minnesota wisely preserved a list of the nativities of its soldiers in the reports of its adjutant-general during the war. Company G, of the Second Regiment, and Companies D and E, of the Fifth Regiment, were both German organizations; and Henning von Minden was captain of Company A of the battalion of cavalry raised by him, and Emil Munch was captain of the First Minnesota Light Artillery. John C. Becht, major of the Fifth Minnesota, and R. von Borgersock, colonel, are among the notable German officers from this State.

Maine had as lieutenant-colonel of its First Artillery Regiment and captain of its Fifth Battery, George F. Leppien, who had been lieutenant in a Pennsylvania battery. He was well known to Philadelphians from his residence and his connection with leading citizens of that city. Educated at a military school in Germany, he showed himself a thorough soldier in his life and in his heroic death.

Michigan supplied four thousand eight hundred and seventy-two Germans out of a total of fourteen thousand foreigners, and in addition to seventy-six thousand native-born citizens, in its portion of the army. It is worth noting that Gould's estimate gives only three thousand five hundred and thirty-four.

In the eleventh and twelfth volumes of *Der Deutsche Pionier*, Cincinnati, 1879-80, are published numerous contributions on the outbreak of the civil war in Missouri, by Friedrich Schnake, which give in great detail the part taken by its German citizens in saving that State for the Union. The leaders of German thought and opinion in St. Louis counted many who afterwards fought for their faith in the ranks of the Union army. Carl Dänzer, Theodore Olshausen, Heinrich Börnstein, and L. C. Bernays, as editors of the *Westlichen Post* and *Anzeiger des Westens*, did much to strengthen their German readers in their political views, and Friedrich Münch, Franz Sigel, Friederich Hecker, and Gustav Koerner gave their powerful help to the cause of the Union. Carl Schurz, Friederich Hassaurek, J. B. Stallo, and others were the leading Republican orators in the war of words that preceded the appeal to arms. Emil Rothe, Egly, Brühl, and Dresel were Douglas Democrats, and Carl Rümelin was spokesman—almost without any German following—for the Breckinridge wing of the party, although the secession lieutenant-governor, Thomas C. Reynolds, was said to be really named Reinhardt, of Prague. A German, Arnold Krekel, now a judge of the United States Court, presided over the convention which forever abolished slavery in Missouri. Blair and Lyon, Schofield and Saxton, were the active representatives of the National Government, but their strength came from the support of the loyal Germans. The Third

Regiment Missouri Volunteers had Franz Sigel for its colonel, the Second, Henry Börnstein. Born in Hamburg in 1801, he entered the Austrian army as a cadet, served in the Italian campaign in 1822, studied medicine in Vienna, was editor, actor, and author in Germany, Austria, Italy, and France, and finally settled in St. Louis after the revolution of 1848, where he established a successful newspaper. Later on he resumed his theatrical undertaking, and then returned to Vienna, where he corresponds with both English and German newspapers in Europe and America. The Fourth Missouri Regiment was commanded by Nicholas Schüttsner, a native of Coblenz, a soldier in the Prussian army, and an emigrant to St. Louis in 1848. One of General Lyon's most useful allies was John J. Witzig, born in Mühlhausen in 1821; educated at Châlons, at the age of nineteen chief engineer of the Paris Orleans Railroad, six years afterwards going to Italy as chief of the construction of the Milan Turin Railroad. In 1849 he came with Cabet's Icarians to Nauvoo, where he remained until 1851, when he came to St. Louis as superintendent of a locomotive works. In 1857 became superintendent of the North Missouri, in 1859 of the Iron Mountain Railroad, remaining in its service until 1865. He died in 1872, member of a large firm of architects and engineers. Another able ally was Captain William Jackson, commander of the German artillery company. His real name was Jacquin. Born in Metz in 1821, he came to the United States in 1834, served three years in the Second United States Dragoons in the Florida and Indian campaigns, was discharged in 1837, enlisted in 1839 in the Third Infantry, and in 1844 in the Seventh, serving under General Taylor in the Mexican war. Settled in St. Louis, he organized in 1852 a company of uhlans, which was afterwards changed to one of dragoons. In 1859 he became captain of the Missouri artillery company, and when the war broke out brought his guns and his company of a hundred men—all Germans except eighteen Frenchmen and Americans—out of the rebel camp into the Union service. He was lieutenant-colonel of the Fifteenth Missouri and captain of the Second Missouri Artillery. One of the captains of Sigel's regiment was Constantin Blandowsky. Born in Prussia, on the border of Russian Poland, in 1821, he was educated at the Polytechnic School in Dresden, served in the French army in Algiers, took part in various unsuccessful Polish revolutions, then fought in Italy against Austria and in the Hungarian army, came to the United States in 1850, and later to St. Louis. He died on May 25, 1861, of wounds received in the attack on Camp Jackson, and was buried with military honors. The work done by the German soldiers of Missouri is told in the history of the war, but the names of those most prominent in their ranks will serve as illustrations of the fitness for the new task laid upon them, and of their loyalty to their new Fatherland.

Peter Joseph Osterhaus was born in Coblenz, studied at the military school in Berlin, and became an officer of the Prussian army. In 1849 he came to the United States, settled in St. Louis, on the outbreak of the civil war was chosen major of the Second Missouri, and after the battle of Wilson's Creek, colonel of the Twelfth Missouri; under Fremont commanded a brigade, at Pea Ridge a division, and on the 9th of June, 1862, was made a brigadier-general. He was assigned the command of a division of the Thirteenth Corps at Helena, and took part in the capture of Arkansas Post on January 13, 1863, and in the subsequent siege of Vicksburg. In the campaigns in Tennessee and Georgia he took a distinguished part; on the 23d July, 1864, was made a major-general, served under General Sherman in the march to the sea, and was chief of staff to General Canby at the surrender of the army of General Kirby Smith, in May, 1865. In 1866 he was appointed American consul in Lyons, France.

Franz Hassendeubel was born at Gernsheim, in Rhenish Bavaria, in 1817, was educated at Speier and Munich, came to the United States in 1842, and settled in St. Louis in 1844. In the Mexican war he was lieutenant in a volunteer battery, and later became captain, and served in New Mexico to the end. At the outbreak of the Rebellion he returned in all speed from Germany, became lieutenant-colonel of Sigel's Third Missouri, constructed the defences of St. Louis, was made brigadier-general, was mortally wounded at the siege of Vicksburg, and died July 17, 1863.

Of the Union forces engaged at the battle of Wilson's Creek, the German organizations were—Osterhaus's battalion, First Kansas Infantry, Colonel Deitzler; Third Missouri, Colonel Franz Sigel; Fifth Missouri, Colonel C. E. Salomon; Colonel Henry Boernstein's regiment, five German regiments from St. Louis, Jefferson City, etc., a light battery of six guns under Lieutenants Schaefer and Schutzenbach, and two batteries of eight guns under Major Backoff.

The Third Regiment of Missouri Volunteers was organized in St. Louis by Franz Sigel for the three months' service, and took part in three battles during that time. The Fourth Regiment was the Black Yaeger Regiment, Colonel Schlittner; the Fifth was also a German regiment, commanded by Colonel Salomon. Of others there were the First Cavalry, Colonel Almstedt; the Second Reserves, Colonel Kallmann; the Third, Colonel Fritz; the Fourth, Colonel Hundehausen and Colonel Wesseling; and the Fifth, Colonel Stifel. Of the three years' regiments there were the Second, Colonel Laibold; the Third, Colonel Hequembourg; the Fourth, Colonel Poten; the Twelfth, Colonel (afterwards General) Osterhaus and Colonel Wangelin; the Fifteenth, Colonel Conrad; the Seventeenth, Colonel Hassendeubel; the Thirty-ninth, Fortieth, and Forty-first, under Kutzner, Weydemeyer, and Von Deutsch, and the Fourth Cavalry, organized out of the Fremont and the Benton Hussars, almost entirely German in its rank and file, although it was commanded by a gallant and able American, Colonel Waring. Von Helmrich, his lieutenant-colonel, was a type of the German soldier.

General Sigel himself was the first rallying-point of the Germans, both of Missouri and the Northwest. Born in Baden in 1824, educated at the military school at Carlsruhe, in command of the republican troops and minister of war in the revolution of 1848, he came to the United States in 1850, lived in New York until 1858, when he went to St. Louis, where he became a teacher in the German-American Academy and editor of a military journal. When the Rebellion broke out he raised the first German regiment; and that old patriot, Hecker, came with his sons from their home in Illinois, enlisted under Sigel, and served with him until Hecker was made colonel of an Illinois regiment. From Wisconsin came General Salomon, who became colonel of the Fifth Missouri, a brigadier-general, and commanded a division in Fremont's army. Sigel's later services are part of the general history of the war of the Rebellion.

In the "Geschichte des 4-jährigen Bürgerkrieges in d. V. S.," von C. Sander, "Hauptman in d. k. pr. Artillerie," Frankfort-am-Main, Sauerländer, 1865, it is stated that of the forty-three thousand officers of the United States forces, from three to four hundred only had been trained in military life abroad; and their services were interfered with by the jealousy of the native citizens, by their ignorance of the language, and of the new conditions of a war in a country in which they were strangers.

These statements are mere generalizations, not based on any precise information, and the best reply to them is found in the facts and names here gathered together.

Carl Schurz was born on the banks of the Rhine, became well known through his active share in the flight of Kinkel, gave up his embassy in Spain to become a general of volunteers, and became a member of Hayes's cabinet. His services as an orator before the war made his name familiar to the whole country, and his return to civil life has been marked by many evidences of popular esteem and affection. As editor of a series of books on our early German history by Kapp and Seidensticker, he has again taken the place which he has so well earned as the type of the German-American citizen, equally loyal to the country of his birth and that of his adoption and his home, and alike appreciated in both.

In Nebraska, the German soldiers did good service in the defence of the borders from Indians, in the Second Cavalry, under General Sully; and in one engagement in Dakota, in September, 1863, the Indians, numbering two thousand warriors, were defeated, but not without a severe loss. When the regiment had served out its time, its veterans were consolidated in an independent battalion of four companies, and assigned to duty on the plains with the First Nebraska Cavalry. In the summer of 1864 the Seventh Iowa Cavalry was assigned the defence of the overland post route from Fort Kearney to the borders,—the First Nebraska Cavalry and a company of regular cavalry continued the line, and protected the country from attacks by the Indians. The raids became more and more frequent and bloody, and hundreds of homes were destroyed, and many settlers and their families killed or captured. The local government organized a force of volunteers, and the War Department strengthened it by such aid as it could give, and thus the country was saved a repetition of the bloody horrors of West Minnesota. The First Veteran Cavalry Regiment was one-half German, and under Lieutenant-Colonel Baümer proved that it was able to cope successfully with the Indians. Almost in sight of sixteen thousand hostiles, he hanged "Black Kettle," an Indian chief, convicted by a court-martial of murder. William Baümer was born in Münster, Prussia, in 1826, was educated there at its High School, was by turns a carver and turner in wood, architect, and a railroad employé. He served three years in the Thirteenth Infantry, saw some active service, came to the United States in 1852, worked in Cincinnati, then settled in Guttenburg, Iowa, went to Dubuque, where he established his reputation as architect and builder, then went to St. Joseph, Missouri; there he joined a German rifle company, at the outbreak of the Rebellion removed to Omaha, joined the First Nebraska, became its captain, served to the end of the war, and died in Omaha in 1869. His name is perpetuated by the Baümer Post, Grand Army of the Republic, of Nebraska City.

New Jersey had no distinctive German regiments, although the Third New Jersey Cavalry, recruited at Hoboken and Jersey City, was largely composed of Germans; but German companies were found in its regiments, notably K of the First, D of the Second, E of the Third, A of the Fourth, and G and L of the Second Cavalry, and K and L of the Third, and Batteries B and C of the First Artillery.

General Mindel, colonel of the Thirty-third New Jersey, was a very gallant and distinguished soldier.

The Third New Jersey Cavalry (or Thirty-sixth New Jersey Regiment) was mustered into service,

February 10, 1864, as the First United States Hussars. Among its officers were Major Siegfried von Forstner, Captains Herzberg, Schafer, Knoblesdorf, and Stoll, Lieutenants Stulpnagel, Kramer, Siebeth, Bulow, Walpel.

Joseph Karge, formerly a Prussian officer, was lieutenant-colonel of the First New Jersey Cavalry, commanded the First Brigade of Grierson's Division of Cavalry, and is now professor at Princeton. General Mindel commanded a brigade consisting of the One Hundred and Twenty-seventh Pennsylvania, the One Hundred and Thirty-fourth New York, and the Thirty-third New Jersey.

Among the familiar names distinguished in the Rebellion is that of the Roeblings, whose services in war have been overshadowed by their brilliant success in civil life; yet their share was no small one in the labors and the glories of the struggle for the Union.

Captain Sohm as an artillerist and General Karge as a cavalry officer, and Major von Forstner and Major Alstrom of the Third New Jersey Cavalry, were among those who did especial service.

Ohio has a large proportion of Germans in its borders, and from them have come many soldiers.

In the Mexican war Cincinnati sent three German companies, Columbus, Dayton, Hamilton, each two, and the Second Ohio Volunteers was called the German Regiment. It was commanded by August Moor, who had served in the Florida war, and who served again in the Rebellion. When Fort Sumter was fired on, three German infantry companies and the Washington Dragoons were on their way to Washington the day the first call for troops was issued. Two German regiments were soon organized, and more than a third of the soldiers from Ohio were Germans. There were eleven German regiments: Ninth, Colonel Kammerling; Twenty-eighth, Colonel Moor; Thirty-seventh, Colonel Sieber; Forty-seventh, Colonel Porschner; Fifty-eighth, Colonel Bausenwein; Sixty-seventh, Colonel Burstenbinder; Seventy-fourth, Colonel von Schrader; One Hundred and Sixth, Colonel Tafel; One Hundred and Seventh, Colonel Meyer; One Hundred and Eighth, Colonel Limberg; One Hundred and Sixty-fifth, Colonel Bohländer; Third Cavalry, Colonel Zahm; three batteries, Hoffman's, Dilger's, and Markgraf's. The German general officers from Ohio were Weitzel, Kautz, Moor, Ammen, von Blessing, Darr, Giese, Leister, Meyer, von Schrader, and Ziegler.

August Moor, colonel of the Twenty-eighth Ohio, was born in Leipsic in 1814, came to this country in 1833, was an officer of the Washington Guard of Philadelphia, and with its captain, Koseritz, took part in the Seminole war in 1836 as lieutenant of a dragoon regiment. In the Mexican war he rose from captain to colonel of the Fourth Ohio, and at the outbreak of the Rebellion was made colonel of the Twenty-eighth Ohio, the second German regiment, and became a brigadier-general as a reward for his gallant service. Von Blessing of the Thirty-seventh Ohio, Degenfeld of the Twenty-sixth, Aug. Dotze of the Eighth Ohio Cavalry, Alex. von Schrader of the Seventy-fourth Ohio, Seidel of the Third Ohio Cavalry, Sondersdorff of the Ninth Ohio, Tafel of the One Hundred and Sixth Ohio, were among those whose services are worth remembering.

General August Willich was born in Gorzyn, in East Prussia, in 1810, of an old noble family; his father had been captain in a hussar regiment. As a child, the son, on the death of his father, became a member of the family of Schleiermacher, the famous theologian,—a connection by marriage. At twelve he was sent to the cadet school at Potsdam. In 1828, after graduating at the military school in

Berlin, he became an officer of an artillery regiment, and in 1841, captain. A Socialist Democrat, he learned the trade of a carpenter in his leisure hours, and, leaving the service, soon took a foremost rank in the revolution of 1848. In 1853 he came to the United States with the idea of organizing a force here to lead against Hamburg and Germany. He found means of livelihood in the navy yard at Brooklyn, then was appointed to the Coast Survey, and finally became editor of the *German Republican* of Cincinnati, where he was living when the Rebellion broke out. He enlisted in the First Ohio, became its adjutant and major of the Ninth Ohio, and later, colonel of the Thirty-second (First German) Indiana; was made a brigadier-general after Shiloh, when his lieutenant-colonel, Von Trebra, became colonel of the regiment. He died January 23, 1878.

Christopher Degenfeld was born in Germany in 1824, and trained there as a soldier. He was major of the Twenty-sixth Ohio Volunteers, and afterwards captain of the Twelfth Ohio Cavalry. His severe wounds obliged him to retire, and his life was shortened by his suffering, until his death, in his fifty-fourth year, in Sandusky.

Captain Hermann Dettweiler was born in Baden in 1825, and was a soldier in its revolutionary army. He served in the Sixth Kentucky until his wounds obliged him to leave the field. He died in Louisville on the 11th of September, 1878.

Battery A, First West Virginia Artillery, Captain Furst, of Wheeling, was composed of Germans.

Wisconsin had for its war governor Edward Salomon, born in Halberstadt, Prussia, in 1828. He came to Wisconsin in 1849, and was by turns schoolteacher, county surveyor, court clerk, lawyer, and governor. The Ninth Wisconsin was raised by Colonel — later General — Frederich Salomon. Born in Prussia in 1826, engineer, architect, and soldier in Germany, he too came to the United States. He first served in a Missouri regiment, but returned to organize a German regiment in Wisconsin. His companies were, among other striking titles, The Sheboygan Tigers, The Sigel Guard, The Wisconsin Tigers, and The Tell Sharpshooters. When the colonel became a brigadier-general, the regiment was commanded by Colonel Jacobi and by Colonel Charles E. Salomon, the third and eldest brother.

Colonel Charles E. Salomon was, like the governor and the general, born in Germany, in

1822. He was educated as a surveyor, served as a volunteer in the Pioniers, and in 1843 became an officer of that corps. He was employed, too, in railroad and other engineering work. In 1849 he came West; in 1850 to St. Louis, where he was elected county surveyor,—defeating Ulysses S. Grant in the contest for the popular vote,—county engineer, and held a variety of other technical offices in the city's service. He organized and was colonel of the Fifth Missouri Volunteers, and when it was mustered out took command of the Ninth Wisconsin, winning the brevet of brigadier-general. Returned to civil life, he was frequently employed by the United States, and died on February 8, 1880.

The Twenty-sixth Wisconsin was another German regiment, organized at Camp Sigel, Milwaukee, and commanded by Colonel Jacobi and General Winkler. It served in the Eleventh Corps, and shared in its varying fortunes in the East and its brilliant successes under Sherman. The Twenty-seventh was also a German regiment under Colonel Conrad Krez, so were the Thirty-fourth, under Colonel Fritz Anneke, and the Thirty-fifth, under Colonel Henry Orff. Gustav von Deutsch commanded a company of cavalry from Wisconsin, which became Company M of the Fourth Missouri Cavalry. The Second Battery, Wisconsin Artillery, was also a German organization. The Fritz Anneke of the Thirty-fourth Wisconsin was also the author of the "Zweite Freiheitsampf," published at Frankfort-on-the-Main, in 1861.

Of the German soldiers in the Rebellion, those mentioned in these pages may well be considered typical examples. These are but a small proportion of the great number who served with equal patriotism. It is not possible in any brief way to give a detailed account of all of those who were fortunate enough to be distinguished in their special services. These pages are only a sketch of the active share taken in every part of the country by its German citizens, and perhaps some more diligent student may yet complete the picture by an exhaustive study of the subject. Imperfect as it is, with all its omissions and shortcomings, it will, however, serve to show that the Germans did their share in the war for the Union, alike in numbers, in courage, in endurance, in zeal, in all the qualities that make the good soldier and the good citizen. They may fairly point with pride to the record of their achievements and claim for them the reward of duty well done. Both those who brought with them the training, skill, and experience acquired in Germany, and those who had as part of their inheritance their national qualities, deserve to be remembered; this will have been successfully done if their names be for even a little while rescued from forgetfulness and oblivion.

There were, of course, on the surface, many Germans who rose early to a dangerous eminence, and some ended their career with anything but credit to themselves or their countrymen, but these were soon thinned out by the actual experiences of real war. As they disappeared, their places were taken by men of merit, and the German soldier earned the rank which his own achievements had gained for him. It was in the ranks, and as non-commissioned officers, that their steadiness, courage, discipline, endurance, and other manly virtues were especially marked. Courage is not such a rare virtue, but the capacity to be a good soldier in the long and weary months of inaction, in the depression incidental to defeat, in the license that follows victory, in the trying hours of imprisonment and sickness,—this was the marked characteristic of the German soldier, and it shone out in those regiments and companies in which the mass was made up of impetuous and undisciplined Americans, unaccustomed to obedience and self-sacrifice. Here and there a German was found who steadied the others by his example, sometimes without a word, occasionally by a little encouragement, always by his manly and soldierly qualities. The literature of the war is largely made up of the heroic achievements of those who gained promotion and distinction, but there is also found in regimental histories and in the dry annals of State records, the occasional mention of some special gallantry of the enlisted man. The story of his part of the hardships and the successes of the war remains to be told,—cannot, perhaps, in view of the vast number of soldiers, ever be fully told,—but wherever the German soldier served, there he made his mark by characteristic virtues, the distinguishing traits of his nationality, in both new and old country.

The Hon. Andrew D. White, lately President of Cornell University, and formerly United States Minister to Germany, gave an admirable summary of the intellectual debt of the United States to Germany in his address, delivered October 4, 1884, at the centennial celebration of the German Society of New York. The title is the key to the note he strikes. It is entitled "Some Practical Influences of German Thought upon the United States," and it is full of suggestive ideas and profound thoughts. He refers to the Revolution, when "the organizing power of Steuben, the devotion of Kalb, and the rude courage of Herckheimer were precious in establishing the liberties of the country;" to the recognition of the infant Republic by Frederic the Great, first of all European rulers; and to the "earnestness of German-American thinkers, so long as the struggle was carried on with the pen, and the bravery of German-American soldiers when it was carried on by the sword." He pays fitting tribute to the words and deeds of sympathy that came from Germany alone in the fearful darkness and distress of the civil war, when "German scholars and thinkers, men like Theodore Mommsen and his compeers, proclaimed their detestation of slavery and their hope for the American Union." In another place he shows the reflex effect of the great work done by a German-American as orator, soldier, and statesman, when, speaking of Carl Schurz as "first of all the recent American thinkers," he tells us that Bismarck said to him, "As a German I am proud of the success of Carl Schurz." He closes in an earnest hope that "the healthful elements of German thought will aid powerfully in evolving a future for this land purer in its politics, nobler in its conception of life, more beautiful in the bloom of art, more precious in the fruitage of character." What the Germans have already done in and for this country is the best assurance that this fervent prayer will be granted. To show their share as soldiers in the wars of the United States, is at least a justification of the right and duty cast upon them to see that so far as in them lies, neither from within nor without shall any injury befall the Republic.

GERMAN OFFICERS OF THE REVOLUTIONARY ARMY.

GENERAL OFFICERS.

DeKalb, John, maj.-gen., 1777.
Steuben, F. W. A., maj.-gen., 1778.
De Woedtke, Frederick William, brig.-gen., 1776.
Muhlenberg, T. P. G., brig.-gen., 1777.
Weedon, George, brig.-gen., 1777.

Weisenfels, F., lieut.-col. com. 4th N. Y., 1779.
Ziegler, D., capt. 1st Penna., 1778.

GERMAN BATTALION.

Weltener, Ludwick, lieut.-col., 1776.
Burchart, D., maj., 1777.
Bunner, J., capt., 1776.
Boyer, P., capt., 1777.
Boetzel, Charles, capt., 1777.
Rice, William, capt., 1778.
Hubley, Bernard, capt., 1778.
Myers, Chr., capt., 1778.
Boyer, Mich., capt., 1778.
Schrauder, Ph., capt., lieut., 1778.
Weidman, John, lieut., 1777.
Sugart, Martin, lieut., 1777.
Gremeth, Jacob, lieut., 1778.
Cramer, Jacob, lieut., 1778.
Swartz, Godfrey, lieut., 1778.
Young, Marcus, lieut., 1778.
Morgan, David, lieut., 1778.

Weidman, John, ens., 1777.
Shrupp, Henry, ens., 1777.
Desenderfer, David, ens., 1778.
Spech, Henry, ens., 1778.
Raboldt, Jacob, ens., 1778.
Glickner, Ch., ens., 1778.
Prue, William, ens., 1778.
Hehn, Henry, ens., 1779.

Independent Corps.

Schott, John Paul, capt., 1776.
Selim, Anthony, capt., 1776.

Invalid Regiment.

Nicola, Lewis, col., 1777.
Woelpper, David, capt., 1778.

Marechausee Light Dragoons.

Van Heer, Barthol., capt., 1778.
Manaeké, Christ., lieut., 1778.
Maitinger, Jac., lieut., 1778.
Struebing, Phil., lieut., 1778.

Armand's Legion, Cavalry.

Markle, Chas., capt., 1778.
Schaffner, George, capt., 1778.
Seibert, Henry, lieut., 1778.
Schwartz, Godfried, lieut., 1778.
Segern, Fred., lieut., 1778.
Riedel, Henry, ens., 1778.

REGULAR ARMY.

Bauman, Sebastian, maj.-com't. Art., 1778.
Kalteisen, Michael, capt. Art., 1794.
Muhlenburg, Henry, lieut. Art., 1794.
Ziegler, David, capt. 1st Inf., 1784.
Strubing, Philip (Van Heer's Corps), capt., bv't., 1784.

The following officers of the regular army were Germans:

Adam, Emil, Alton Jägers, 1861; capt. 9th Ill., 1861; major 114th Ill., 1865; capt. 5th U. S. Cav., 1870.
Adolphus, Philip, Prussia; surgeon, 1861–65; Md.
Axt, Godfrey H. T., Germany; surgeon 20th N. Y. Vols.; U. S. A., 1867.
Balder, Christian, enl. U. S. A. May 12, 1857; 1st lieut. 25th Inf., 1862.
Bendire, Charles, enl. U. S. A., 1854; capt. 1st Cav., 1873; retired 1886.
Bentzoni, Charles, enl. U. S. A., 1857; col. 56th U. S. Col. Troops, 1865; capt. 25th Inf., 1866.
Clous, John W., enl. U. S. A , 1857; capt. 24th Inf., 1867.
Conrad, Joseph, capt. 3d Mo., 1861; col. 15th Mo., 1862; capt. 11th Inf., 1869; retired as colonel, 1882.
Crone, L. E., 22d Mass., 1861; capt. 42d Inf., 1866; retired 1870.
Decker, Th., 4th Art., 1875; 2d lieut. 24th Inf., 1879.
De Gress, Jacob C., capt. 6th Mo. Cav.; capt. 9th U. S. Cav., 1867; retired 1870.
Ebstein, F. H. E., enl. U. S. A., 1864; capt. 21st Inf., 1885.
Eggenmeyer, A., 1st lieut. 12th Inf.; killed June 1, 1864.

Falck, William, enl. 1858; capt. 2d Inf., 1866; retired 1883.

Freudenberg, C. G., capt. 52d N. Y., 1861; capt. 14th Inf., 1869; retired as lieut.-col., 1877.

Fuger, F., enl. 4th Art., 1856; 1st lieut., 1865.

Gaebel, F., 1st lieut. 45th Inf., 1866.

Gardener, Corn., 2d lieut. 19th Inf., 1879.

Gerlach, William, enl. 1856; 1st lieut. 3d Inf., 1879.

Goldman, H. J., 2d lieut. 5th Cav., 1877.

✓ Green, John, enl. July 1, 1846; maj. 1st Cav., 1868; lieut.-col. 2d Cav., 1885.

Grossman, F. E., 2d lieut. 7th Inf., 1863; capt. 17th Inf., 1871.

Gunther, S., enl. 1st Cav., 1855; capt. 4th Cav., 1870; retired 1884.

Heger, A., surgeon U. S. A., 1856-67.

von Hermann, C. J., maj. A. A. D. C; capt. 4th Inf., 1866.

Hesselberger, G. A., 2d lieut., 1866; 1st lieut. 3d Inf., 1871.

Hoelcke, William, German army, 1849-51; British Legion in Crimea; 1st lieut. Mo. Vols.; 1st lieut. 39th U. S., 1866-70.

Hoffman, Ernest F., Royal Engineers, Berlin; lieut. Prussian army, 1844-56; capt. and maj. Italian army; 2d lieut. 35th Inf., 1867.

Hoppy, E., enl. 2d Art., 1854; 1st lieut. 9th Inf., 1871; retired.

Ilges, Guido, 14th Inf., 1861; lieut.-col. 9th Inf., 1871.

Johnson, Lewis, 10th Ind., 1861; bvt. brig.-gen. U. S. Vols., 1865; capt. 24th Inf., 1869.

Kautz, A. V., 1st Ohio, 1846; 2d lieut. 4th Inf., 1852; capt. 6th Cav., 1861; col. 2d Ohio Cav., 1862; brig.-gen. Vols., 1864; bvt. maj.-gen., 1865; col. 8th Inf., 1874.

Keller, J. W., 6th Mass., 1861; 1st lieut. 42d Inf., 1866; capt. retired list, 1870.

Keye, F., 2d lieut. 10th Inf., 1869.

Koerper, E. A., surgeon 75th Pa., U. S. A., 1867.

Kopp, William, 1st lieut. Washington Territory Vols., 1862; 1st lieut. 13th Inf., 1867.

Kramer, A., 2d Dragoons, 1857; capt. 15th Penna. Cav., 1862; capt. 6th Cav., 1874.

⌐ Kroutinger, A. W., enl. 2d Inf., 1848; capt. 2d Inf., 1864; retired 1879.

Liedtke, F. W., 11th Penna., 1861; 2d lieut. 43d Inf., 1866; 1st Inf., 1871.

Lockwood, T. A., 2d lieut. 17th Inf., 1880.

von Luettwitz, A. H., 54th N. Y., 1862; 1st lieut. 3d Cav., 1874; retired 1879.

Luhn, G. L., enl. 1853; capt. 4th Inf., 1875.

Magnitzky, G., 20th Mass., 1861; capt., 1864; 2d lieut. 14th Inf., 1870; retired 1871.

Mahnken, John H., 1st N. Y. Cav.; 1st lieut. 8th U. S. Cav., 1877.

Meinhold, Charles, 3d Cav., 1862; capt. 3d Cav., 1866; died 1877.

Merkle, Charles F., 1st lieut. 4th Art., 1862.

Meyer, Martin, capt. 12th Inf., 1861.

Meyers, Edward, 2d lieut. 1st Cav., 1862; 7th Cav., 1866.

Michaelis, O. E., 23d N. Y.; capt. Ordnance, 1874.

von Michalowsky, T. B., 2d lieut. 1st Art., 1861; 1st lieut., 1863.

Motz, John, 1st lieut. 11th Inf., 1847.

Orlemann, L. H., 103d, and capt. 119th N. Y.; 1st lieut. 10th Cav., 1867; retired 1879.

Patzki, J. H., surgeon 15th N. Y.; capt. asst. surg. U. S. A., 1869.

Paulus, Jacob, 5th and 50th Penna.; 2d lieut. 18th U. S. Inf.; capt. 25th Inf., 1873.

Phisterer, F., 2d lieut. 18th Inf., 1861; capt. 36th Inf. and 7th Inf., 1869.

Rawolle, W. C., 2d lieut. 2d N. Y. Art., 1861; 2d lieut. 2d Cav., 1868; adjt., 1878; capt., 1880.

Reichmann, Carl, enl. 1881; 2d lieut. 24th Inf., 1884.
Renaldo, H. O., 2d lieut. 9th Inf., 1861; 1st lieut., 1863.
Rendlebrock, J., enl. 1851; 2d lieut. 4th Cav., 1862; capt., 1867; retired 1879.
Ritzius, H. P., 5th N. Y., 1861; maj. 52d N. Y., 1864; 1st lieut. 25th Inf., 1875.
Roemer, Paul, enl. 5th Art., 1858; 1st lieut., 1866.
Ruhlen, George, 1st lieut. 17th Inf., 1876.
Quentin, J. E., capt. 103d N. Y.; 1st lieut. 14th Inf., 1867.
Sachs, H., 2d lieut. 3d Cav., 1861.
Schaurte, F. W., 2d lieut. 2d Cav., 1862; capt., 1866.
von Schirach, F. C., 54th N. Y., 1861; 1st lieut. 43d Inf., 1866; retired 1870.
von Schrader, Alexander, 2d lieut. 11th Inf., 1866; maj. 39th Inf., 1866; died 1867.
Schreyer, George, 2d lieut. 6th Cav., 1866.
Schultze, Thilo, 12th Mo., 1865; 2d lieut. 14th Inf., 1865.
Schwann, Theo., enl. 1857; capt. 11th Inf., 1866.
Sellmer, Charles, enl. 1854; capt. 11th Me., 1862; 1st lieut. 3d Art., 1877.
Simon, Charles, 2d lieut. 5th Art., 1862; 1st lieut., 1866.
Smith, John E., col. 45th Ill.; col. 27th Inf., 1866; retired 1881.
Smith, Thos., enl. 1867; 1st lieut. 15th Inf., 1877.
Steinmetz, William R., capt. and asst. surg., 1871.
Stelyes, Claus, 2d lieut. 4th Art., 1863.
Sternberg, Sig., 2d lieut. 27th Inf.; killed 1867.
Stiebner, Eugene; army, 1st Art. Fort Sumter, 1861; 1st New York Art., 1862; 3d Penna., 1863; 16th N. Y., 1864; 2d lieut. 15th Inf., 1865; 1st lieut. 33d Inf.
Stommel, Julius, 41st N. Y.; 2d lieut. 43d Inf., 1866; 1st lieut., 1869.

Syberg, Arnold, capt. 11th Inf., 1847.
Thibaut, F. W., 2d lieut. 7th N. Y., 1861; 1st lieut. 6th Inf., 1868.
Thies, F., enl. 1866; 2d lieut. 3d Inf., 1873.
Urban, Gustavus, army; 2d lieut. 5th Cav.; capt., 1866.
Valois, Gustavus, capt. 4th Md., 1862; capt. 9th Cav., 1884.
Veitenheimer, Carl, 74th Penna.; 2d lieut. 4th Inf.; 1st lieut., 1866.
Vermann, Otto, 2d lieut. 13th Inf., 1866.
Wagner, Henry, enl. 1856; 2d lieut. 11th Inf., 1863; capt. 1st Cav., 1869.
Walbach, John de B., 1st lieut. Cav., 1799; col. 4th Art., 1842; died, 1857.
Warrens, C. N., 1st lieut. 4th Mo., 1861; capt. 14th Inf., 1883.
Wedemeyer, W. G., enl. 1861; capt. 16th Inf., 1865.
Wenckebach, E. F., 2d lieut. 13th Inf., 1865; capt. 22d Inf., 1867.
Wesendorff, Max, 1st lieut. Washington Territory Vols., 1862; 2d lieut. 24th Inf., 1867; capt. 1st Cav., 1880.
Wilhelmi, Louis, 2d lieut. 1st Inf., 1865; 1st lieut., 1880.

The following, from a "List of Field Officers ot U. S. Volunteers," are Germans:

Abell, Caspar K., maj. 72d N. Y.
Abell, Charles C., maj. 6th N. Y. and 10th N. Y. Art.
Almstedt, Henry, col. 1st Mo.; 2d Mo. Lt. Art.
Alstrom, John V., maj. 3d N. J. Cav.
Ammen, Jacob, col. 12th Ohio.
von Amsberg, George, col. 45th N. Y.
Anselm, Albert, lieut.-col. 3d Mo.
Arn, F., maj. 31st Ind.
Balling, O. H. P., maj. 145th N. Y.

Banghof, C., maj. 1st Mo. Cav.
von Baumbach, C., maj. 24th Wis.
Bausenwein, V., col. 58th Ohio.
Becht, John C., maj. 5th Minn.
Beck, Arnold, lieut.-col. 2d Mo.
Beck, Christian, lieut.-col. 9th Ind. Cav.
Beck, Fred, maj. 108th Ohio.
Beck, William, maj. 27th Mo.
Becker, Adolph, lieut.-col. 46th N. Y.
Becker, Gottfried, lieut.-col. 28th Ohio.
Becker, Philip, lieut.-col. 5th Penna. Cav.
Behlendorff, F., maj. 13th Ill.
Bendix, John E., col. 7th N. Y.
Bierbower, F., maj. 40th Ky.
Blenker, L., col. 8th N. Y.
von Blessing, L., lieut.-col. 37th Ohio.
von Boernstein, Shaeffer, col. 5th Iowa Cav.
von Borgersock, R., col. 5th Minn.
Botchfur, Hugo, maj. 1st Ark. Cav.
Bramlich, Charles, maj. 2d Ark. Inf.
Brutsche, John D., lieut.-col. 8th Mo. Cav.
Burger, Louis, col. 5th N. Y.
Degenfeld, Christian, col. 26th Ohio.
Deitzler, George W., col. 1st Kansas.
Diechman, Julius, maj. 15th N. Y. Heavy Art.
Dotze, Aug., lieut.-col. 8th Ohio Cav.
Duysing, Emil, lieut.-col. 41st N. Y.
von Egloffstein, F. W., col. 103d N. Y.
Ehrler, Francis, lieut.-col. 2d Mo.
von Einsidel, D., lieut.-col. 41st N. Y.

Erdelmeyer, F., lieut.-col. 32d Ind.
Ernenwein, C., lieut.-col. 21st Penna.
Faltz, Ernst M., lieut.-col. 8th Md.
von Forstner, S., maj. 3d N. J. Cav.
Gaebel, F. A. H., maj. 7th N. Y.
Gellman, F., lieut.-col. 58th N. Y.
von Gerber, G., lieut.-col. 6th Ind.
Glapcke, Herman, maj. 22d Conn.
Goelzer, Aug., lieut.-col. 60th Ind.
Gruesel, Nich., col. 7th Ill.
von Hammerstein, H., col. 78th N. Y.
Happel, Christian, lieut.-col. 10th Mo.
von Hartung, Adolph, col. 74th Penna.
Hassendeubel, F., col. 3d Mo.
Heinrichs, Gust., lieut.-col. 4th Mo. Cav.
Heintz, R., maj. 28th Ohio.
Heintzleman, M. T., lieut.-col. 172d Penna.
von Helmrich, G., lieut.-col. 5th Mo. Cav.
Hequembourg, A. G., lieut.-col. 40th Mo.
Hequembourg, W. A., maj. 3d Mo.
Hundhausen, Julius, lieut.-col. 4th Mo.
Hundhausen, Robert, col. 4th Mo.
Jacobsen, Aug., lieut.-col. 27th Mo.
Jaensch, F., maj. 31st Mo.
Jussen, Edm., lieut.-col. 23d Wis.
Kaercher, Jac., lieut.-col. 12th Mo.
Kahler, F. M., maj. 62d Ohio.
Kammerling, Gus., col. 9th Ohio.
von Kielmansegge, E., col. 4th Mo. Cav.; 1st Florida Cav.
Knobellsdorff, Charles, col. 44th Ill.

Knoderer, Charles, col. 167th Penna.
von Koerber, V. E., maj. 1st Md. Cav.
Koltes, John A., col. 73d Penna.
Kozlay, E. A., col. 54th N. Y.
Krekel, Arnold, maj. Mo. Batt'y.
Kreutzer, William, lieut.-col. 98th N. Y.
Krez, Cornel., col. 27th Wis.
Kummell, A. H., lieut.-col. 13th Wis.
von Kusserow, C., lieut.-col. 2d U. S. Vet. Vols.
Laiboldt, Bernard, col. 2d Mo.
Landgraeber, Clemens, maj. 2d Mo. Lt. Art.
Ledergerber, F. T., maj. 12th Mo.
Leppien, George F., lieut.-col. 1st Me. Art.
Mahler, F., col. 75th Penna.
von Matzdorff, A., lieut.-col. 75th Penna.
Mehler, Adolph, lieut.-col. 98th Penna.
Metternich, G., lieut.-col. 46th N. Y.
Minden, von Henning, maj. Hatch's Batt'n. Minn. Cav.
von Mitzel, Alex., lieut.-col. 74th Penna.
Moor, Aug., col. 28th Ohio.
Mueller, Charles, lieut.-col. 107th Ohio.
Osterhaus, P. J., col. 12th Mo.
Perczel, N., col. 10th Iowa.
Porchner, F., col. 47th Ohio.
Possegger, F., maj. 1st N. Y. Cav.
Reichard, F. H., maj. 188th Penna.
Reichard, George N., lieut.-col. 143d Penna.
Rolshausen, F., maj. 82d Ill.
Rosa, Rudolph, col. 46th N. Y.
Rosengarten, Adolph G., maj. 15th Penna. (Anderson) Cav.

Salm-Salm, Prince, col. 8th N. Y.
von Schach, G. W., col. 7th N. Y.
Schadt, Otto, lieut.-col. 12th Mo.
Schaeffer, F., col. 2d Mo.
von Schickfus, F., lieut.-col. 1st N. Y. Cav.
von Schilling, F., maj. 3d Penna. Art.
Schimmelfennig, A., col. 74th Penna.
Schirmer, L., col. 15th N. Y.
Schlittner, Nich., col. 4th Mo.
von Schluembach, Alex., maj. 29th N. Y.
Schnepf, E., lieut.-col. 20th N. Y.
Schoeffel, F. A., lieut.-col. 13th N. Y.
von Schrader, Alex., lieut.-col. 74th Ohio.
Schumacher, F., maj. 21st Wis.
Segebarth, H., maj. 3d Penna. Art.
Seidel, C. B., col. 3d Ohio Cav.
Seidel, G. A., maj. 7th N. Y.
Seidlitz, Hugo, maj. 27th Penna.
Soest, Clemens, col. 29th N. Y.
Sondersdorff, C., lieut.-col. 9th Ohio.
Stahel, Julius, col. 8th N. Y.
von Steinhausen, A., lieut.-col. 68th N. Y.
von Steinwehr, A., col. 29th N. Y.
Tafel, Gust., lieut.-col. 106th Ohio.
Tassin, A. G., col. 35th Ind.
Thielemann, Christian, col. 16th Ill. Cav.
Thielemann, Milo, maj. 16th Ill. Cav.
Thoman, Max, lieut.-col. 59th N. Y.
Tiedemann, D. F., lieut.-col. 110th U. S. Colored.
von Trebra, H., col. 32d Ind.

von Vegesach, E., col. 20th N. Y.
Veitenheimer, Carl, lieut.-col. 74th Penna.
Wagner, Louis, col. 88th Penna.
Wangelin, Hugo, col. 12th Mo.
Weber, Max, col. 20th N. Y.
von Wedell, Carl, maj. 68th N. Y.
Willich, A., col. 32d Ind.
Zakrzenski, H., lieut.-col. 2d Mo.

INDEX.

Adenbousch, 2d Va., 85.
Almstedt, 1st Mo. Cav., 141.
Alstrom, 3d N. J., 146.
Amsberg, von, 45th N. Y., 115.
Ammen, 24th O., 62.
Annecke, 23d, 34th Wis., 151.
Anspach, 38.
Armlinsen, von, N. O. Turner Guards, 85.
Arndt, 1st N. Y. Art., 126.
Asboth, 93.

Bachman, W. K., S. C., 83.
Bachman's Battery, Washington Art., C. S. A., 85.
Bahncke, N. O. Turner Guards, 85.
Ballier, 98th Pa., 106.
Baltzel, C., 23.
Bauman, Col., U. S. A., 25, 38.
Baumer, 1st Neb., 145.

Bausenwein, 58th Ohio, 147.
Becht, J. C., 5th Minn., 135.
Becker, 50.
Bendix, Col., 7th N. Y., 114.
Biebel, 6th Conn., 133.
Bierbower, 40th Ky., 134.
Bierer, E., 171st Pa., 107.
Blandowsky, 3d Mo., 138.
Blankenburg, H., 77.
Blenker, 93, 123.
Blessing, von, L., 37th Ohio, 148.
Boernstein, 2d Mo., 137.
Bohländer, 115th Ohio, 147.
Bohlen, H., 75th Pa., 110.
Boone, Daniel, 35.
Borcke, von, Heros, C. S. A., 76.
Borgersock, 135.
Bouquet, 12.
Brickel, 1st N. Y. Lt. Art., 125.
Brueckner, 73d Pa., 111.
Buggenhagen, von, 7th N.Y., 121.

Bunner, R., 23d Continental, 50.
Burckhart, D., 23.
Burger, 5th N. Y. S. M., 115.
Burger, N. O. Steuben Guards, 85.
Burstenbinder, 67th Ohio, 147.
Bushbeck, A., 27th Pa., 109.

Closen, von, 42.
Colorado, 126.
Connecticut, 133.
Conrad, A., 77, 44.
Cordes, T., S. C., 81.
Cornehlsen, N. C., 79.
Cramer, J., 23.
C. S. A., 85.
Custer, Gen. George, 68.

Degenfeld, C., 26th Ohio, 149.
Demler, 38.
Dettweiler, H., 6th Ky., 150.
Deutsch, von, 4th Mo. Cav., 152.
Dieterich, 1st N. Y. Lt. Art., 125.
Dilger, Ohio, 147.
Doster, 4th Pa. Cav., 108.
Dotze, 8th Ohio Cav., 148.
Dreer, F. J., 25.

Eickhoff, 78.
Elking, von, 19.
Engelmann, 43d Ill., 127.

Ermentrout, Daniel, 10.
Esebeck, 41.
Estvan, 77.
Ewald, 42.

Farmer, 50.
Fersen, 42.
Forstner, von, 3d N. J. Cav., 146.
Frank, 52d N. Y., 115.
Freilich, 38.
Freudenberg, 52d N. Y., 117.
Frey, 24th Ill., 131.
Fry, Gen. J. B., 88.
Furman, 38.
Furst, 1st W. Va. Art., 150.

Gardiner, J. de B. W., U. S. A., 60.
Gau, 42.
Gaudain, von, A., 132.
Georgia, 85.
Gerber, J., 24th Ind., 134.
Gilsa, von, 41st N. Y., 115, 124.
Glichner, Ch., 23.
Gould, Dr. B. A., 89.
Greble, Lieut. J. T., 2d U. S. Art., 69.
Greble, Lieut. E. S., 2d U. S. Art., 71.
Green, G. W., 19.

INDEX.

Gremeth, J., 23.
Gries, 104th Pa., 105.
Griesinger, T., 87.
Gumbart, Ill. Batt., 129.

Haake, 41.
Haake, von, Count, 52d N. Y., 122.
Haas, de, J. P., 41, 50.
Haas, de, W., 43.
Hagner, Gen., 62.
Hambright, Gen. H. A., 73.
Harms, Capt. H., S. C., 81.
Hartmann, J. A., 48.
Hartranft, Gen. J. F., 51st Pa., 107.
Hassendeubel, Col., 17th Mo., 140.
Haupt, Gen. H., 62.
Haussegger, 39.
Hecker, F., 82d Ill., 129.
Heer, van B., 40.
Hehn, 23.
Heileman, J. F., 61.
Heine, W., 103d N. Y., 71.
Heintzelman, Gen. S. P., 62.
Helmrich, von, 4th Mo. Cav., 141.
Hendricks, 1st N. Y. Cav., 122.
Hendricks, W., 24.

Henry, 24.
Herkimer, Gen., 48.
Hiester, 47, 50.
Hofmann, Gen. J. W., 56th Pa., 109.
Hoffman, Ohio Batt., 147.
Howelman, 46.
Hubley, B , 23.

Illinois, 99, 127.
Indiana, 133.
Iowa, 132.

Jackson, William, 3d Mo., 138.
Jacobi, 9th Wis., 151.
Jaulmann, 38.
Jeffereys, 12.
Jenkins, H. M., 40.

Kalb de, Gen., 19, 25.
Kalteisen, M., S. C. Cont'l Art., 32, 33, 35.
Kapff, 7th N. Y., 114.
Kapp, F., 15.
Karge, Gen. J., 1st N. J. Cav., 146.
Kautz, A. V., 8th U. S. Inf., 67.
Kentucky, 134.
Kielmansegge, von, 4th Mo. Cav., 134.

Klein, 6th Conn., 133.
Kleisser, 30th N. Y., 126.
Klingelhoffer, C. S. A., Ark., 55.
Kloch, Col. J., N. Y. Cont'l Reg., 48.
Knierim, 1st N. Y. Art., 125.
Knobelsdorff, von, 44th Ill., 127.
Knoderer, 168th Pa., 106.
Koerber, von, 1st Mo., 134.
Kohler, 98th Pa., 105.
Koltes, 73d Pa., 111.
Körner, G., 35, 128.
Kramer, 3d N. J. Cav., 146.
Krez, Col., 27th Wis., 151.
Kusserow, von, 32d N. Y. Batt., 125.

Lange, A., Inda., 134.
Langenheim, William, 72.
Lederer, John, 79.
Lehmann, 103d Pa., 107.
Leppien, 1st Me. Art., 121.
Lieber, F., 63.
Limberg, 108th Ohio, 147.
Louisiana, 84.
Lowell, E. J., 19.
Loyal Legion, 117.
Luther, 62.
Lutterloh, 35, 37.
Lutz, J. B., 134.

Maine, 135.
Mangold, 78.
Markgraf, Ohio Art., 147.
Marschall, 53.
Matthes, Ia., 132.
Melchers, C. S. A., 80.
Mentges, 50.
Meyer, 107th Ohio, 147.
Michigan, 135.
Mindel, G., 33d N. J., 145.
Minden, von, Henning, Minn. Cav., 134.
Minnesota, 134.
Missouri, 95, 136.
Moegling, 11th Conn., 133.
Moltke, von, 1st N. Y. Cav., 122.
Moor, Aug., 28th Ohio, 147, 148.
Mordecai, Maj., U. S. A., 67.
Mordecai, Col., U. S. A., 68.
Morgan, D., 23.
Muehleck, 73d Pa., 111.
Muhlenberg, 16, 34, 51, 62.

Nast, Thomas, 119.
Nauman, Col. George, U. S. A., 61.
Nebraska, 143.
Neslett, 38.
New Jersey, 145.

New York, 48, 98, 114.
Nohrden, C. S. A., 81.
North Carolina, 79.

Ohio, 99, 147.
Orff, H., 35th Wis., 151.
Osband, Ill. Art., 129.
Osterhaus, 12th Mo., 139.
Ottendorff, 46.

Parkman, F., 13.
Passegger, 1st N. Y. Cav., 122.
Pennsylvania, 8, 10, 13, 100.
Pennypacker, Gen., 97th Pa., 103.
Perczel, A., 10th Iowa, 132.
Pionier, 34, 135,
Poe, 44.
Porschner, 47th Ohio, 147.
Post, C. F., 14.
Provost, 12.
Prux, 23.

Quitman, Gen. J. A., 53.

Raboldt, 23.
Radowitz, von, 121.
Raith, Julius, 43d Ill., 127.
Ratterman, 41.
Riedesel, 19, 49.
Roland, 62.

Rosengarten, A. G., 15th Pa. Cav., 3.
Runge, N. C., 79.
Rüstow, 78.

Salm-Salm, Princess, 120.
Salm-Salm, 8th N. Y., 121.
Salomon, F., 9th Wis.; C. E., 5th Mo.; E. S., 82d Ill., 150, 151.
Sanitary Commission, 89.
Sauer, 20.
Schaefer, de Boernstein, 5th Ia. Cav., 132.
Schach, von, 7th N. Y., 114.
Schall, 51st Pa., 105.
Scheibert, 76.
Scheppert, 33.
Scherer, 121st Pa., 102.
Schickfuss, von, 1st N. Y. Cav., 121.
Schlattler, 13.
Schleicher, Gust., 72, 86.
Schnake, 135.
Schneider, 10.
Schott, J. P., 40.
Schott, 73d Pa., 111.
Schott, 24.
Schirmer, N. Y. Batt., 121.
Schroder, von, 74th Ohio, 39th U. S. A., 73.

Schulz, S. C. Art., 86.
Schurz, 1st N. Y. Cav., 47, 121.
Schütts, 4th Mo. Vols., 137.
Schwarz, 2d Ill. Art., 129.
Schwarzwalder, 5th N. Y. S. M., 115.
Schwenke, 121.
Seidensticker, 39, 49,
Selim. 24.
Shiras, 62.
Shriver, 62.
Shrupp, 23.
Siebath, 3d N. J. Cav., 146.
Sieber, 37th Ohio, 147.
Sigel, F., 3d Mo., 142.
Sigwald, C. B., S. C., 81.
South Carolina, 79.
Stedingk, 42.
Steinwehr von, 29th N. Y., 123.
Steuben, Gen., 19, 20, 31, 37.
Steuben, Baron, von, 52d N. Y., 116.
Stolleman, Ill. Art., 129.
Sugart, 23.
Swartz, 23.
Sytez, George, 38.

Tafel, 106th Ohio, 147.
Texas, 84.
Thayer, 13.

Thielemann, Ill. Cav., 129.
Ticbout, 38.
Tiedeman, 75th Pa., 113.
Trebra, von, 32d Ind., 121.

Vezin, 5th Pa., 15th Pa., 4th Mo. 111.
Virginia, 84.
Voegelin, 1st N. Y. Art., 125.
Vollers, N. C., 79.

Wagener, J. A., S. C. Vols., 72, 81.
Wagner, Gen. L , 88th Pa., 113.
Walbach, 4th U. S. Art., 55.
Wangelin, H., 12th Mo., 128.
Waring, 4th Mo. Cav., 94, 141.
Weber, M., 20th N. Y., 115.
Weedon, Gen., 45.
Weidman, 23.
Weiser, Conrad, 10, 15.
Weissenfels, 36, 38.
Weitzel, Gen. G., 72.
Weltner, 23.
Wetzel, M., 38.
Wetzel, L., 43.
White, A. D., 154
Willich, Gen., 1st German, Ohio; 1st German, Ind.; 32d Ind., 133, 148.

Wisconsin, 99, 150.
Wistar, 108.
Witzig, 137.
Woedtke, von, 34.
Woelpper, Pa. German Reg., 1776, 39.

Zahm, 3d Ohio Cav., 147.
Zedwitz, von, 49.
Ziegler, Pa. Continental Reg., 32.
Zinn, 130th Pa., 105.

THE END.

www.ingramcontent.com/pod-product-compliance
Lightning Source LLC
Chambersburg PA
CBHW022112160426
43197CB00009B/996